W9-CCH-003

# POWER,
# TRUTH,
## AND
# COMMUNITY
## IN
# MODERN
# CULTURE

# Christian Mission and Modern Culture

EDITED BY
ALAN NEELY, H. WAYNE PIPKIN,
AND WILBERT R. SHENK

In the Series:

# POWER,
# TRUTH,
## AND
# COMMUNITY
## IN
# MODERN
# CULTURE

CHARLES C. WEST

TRINITY PRESS
INTERNATIONAL
HARRISBURG, PENNSYLVANIA

Trinity Press International, P.O. Box 1321, Harrisburg, PA 17105

Trinity Press International is a division of The Morehouse Group.

Cover design: Brian Preuss

**Library of Congress Cataloging-in-Publication Data**
West, Charles C.
    Power, truth, and community in modern culture / Charles C. West.
        p. cm. — (Christian mission and modern culture)
    Includes bibliographical references.
    ISBN 1-56338-297-0   (pbk. : alk. paper)
    1. Church and the world.   I. Title.   II. Series.
BR115.W6W47    1999
261—dc21                                                    99–37888
                                                                    CIP

*Printed in the United States of America*

99   00   01   02   03   04   6   5   4   3   2   1

For Ruth,
Companion, Guide, Inspiration

*"So faith, hope and love abide.*
*But the greatest of these is love."*

# Contents

# Preface to the Series

Both Christian mission and modern culture, widely regarded as antagonists, are in crisis. The emergence of the modern mission movement in the early nineteenth century cannot be understood apart from the rise of technocratic society. Now, at the end of the twentieth century, both modern culture and Christian mission face an uncertain future.

One of the developments integral to modernity was the way the role of religion in culture was redefined. Whereas religion had played an authoritative role in the culture of Christendom, modern culture was highly critical of religion and increasingly secular in its assumptions. A sustained effort was made to banish religion to the backwaters of modern culture.

The decade of the 1980s witnessed further momentous developments on the geopolitical front with the collapse of communism. In the aftermath of the breakup of the system of power blocs that dominated international relations for a generation, it is clear that religion has survived even if its institutionalization has undergone deep change and its future forms are unclear. Secularism continues to oppose religion, while technology has emerged as a major source of power and authority in modern culture. Both confront Christian faith with fundamental questions.

The purpose of this series is to probe these developments from a variety of angles with a view to helping the church understand its missional responsibility to a culture in crisis. One important resource is the church's experience of two centuries of cross-cultural mission that has reshaped the church into a global Christian *ecumene.* The focus of our inquiry will be the church in modern culture. The series (1) examines modern/postmodern culture from a missional point of view; (2) develops the theological agenda that the church in modern culture must address in order to recover its own integrity; and (3) tests fresh conceptualizations of the nature and mission of the church as it engages modern culture. In other words, these volumes are intended to be a forum where conventional assumptions can be challenged and alternative formulations explored.

This series is a project authorized by the Institute of Mennonite Studies, research agency of the Associated Mennonite Biblical Seminary, and supported by a generous grant from the Pew Charitable Trusts.

*Editorial Committee*

ALAN NEELY
H. WAYNE PIPKIN
WILBERT R. SHENK

# Introduction
## The Gospel and Our Culture

Christians face an awesome mission at the dawn of the twenty-first century. It is no less than to discern and respond to the ways of God for the society around us. It is our business, in other words, to grasp history—our history—theologically and to act in it with confidence and hope. If we succeed, we will be faithful witnesses and the church will prosper, whatever its external fortunes may be. If we fail, we will simply become part, a religious part to be sure, of an increasingly confused generation.

The mission is clear. It is not easy. We are human. We live by our desires and fears. We depend on our own power and are threatened by the power of others. We absolutize our perspectives and interests. We live from our cultural loyalties and prejudices. In our pride and our anxiety we exalt all of these things—make little gods of them (*idols* was the biblical word)—as we struggle for ultimate truth and security.

We seek that ultimate in many ways. We European-Americans are great self-analysts. The less certain we feel, the more vigorously we seek objective information about our politics, our economy, our cultures, our families, our morals, and our religion—information that will help us to master and control our fate. We are great moralists. Americans especially love to define ourselves by moral standards that reflect our own good conscience, while we claim that they are the law for all. Then, when challenged, we seek still more universal principles by which to judge and justify our idealized selves and societies. Moreover, most of us are religious seekers as well. We yearn for some meaningful reality that transcends this world, that relieves our anxieties and fulfills our deepest desires. But we not only seek; we project and define such a reality according to our own needs, experiences, and hopes. We even press Deity, however we define it, into the service of our religious enterprise. We find it hard to *begin* with God.

Dietrich Bonhoeffer described our predicament thus:

> Our thinking… the thinking of fallen men and women, has no beginning because it is a circle. We think in a circle. We feel and will in a circle. We exist in a circle. We… find we are in the middle, knowing neither the end nor the beginning, and yet knowing that we are in the middle, coming from the beginning and going toward the end. We see that our life is determined by these two facets, of which we know only that we do not know them (1989:26–27, my trans.; cf. 1997:26, 28).

All this self-centered circularity crowds in on us as we try to cope with reality and distorts our minds. Who are we really, in this our culture, before God? How can truth break through our defenses with a defining word that we could not speak to ourselves? How does God intervene to guide us toward social and personal self-understanding? By what authority, to what hope, are we called amid the forces that are driving our history? To these questions this book is devoted.

Who then is God? What is the gospel? The question is not metaphysical, moral, or religious. It is not the goal of a human search or the fulfillment of a human experience, as if we could define and use Deity according to our concepts and desires. It can be answered only in response to a self-revealing God. We human beings are not our own creators. We are not the subjects of our knowledge, the authors of our goodness, or the masters of our spirituality. We are not the center of our existence. Our power does not control our destiny. We think, we act, we live in the middle of life, not knowing our beginning or end, but only that we are created and called to be in the middle. We are limited by the other person with whom we are called to live and by the Creator who has made us, whose word gives our life meaning and direction. That this middle and this limit are grace perfected in love, we know from Jesus Christ, who shared them with us and redeemed them with his death and resurrection. That we can live in them with joy and hope, we know from the work of the Holy Spirit among us.

But these trinitarian relationships are more than a formula. They express the long history of God's covenant love, justice, and faithfulness toward a rebellious and self-centered people, first among the Hebrews, then among all the nations. They describe the God whose victory in Christ over the powers of sin and death in this world we call gospel or, in the original Greek, good news. The context of theology is faith—trust in this

God to lead us into truth, love—being forgiven and transformed by the One who loves us, and hope—discernment of and action toward the future that God has promised for us and the world under the reign of Christ. This is the reality for twenty-first century America that we all are invited to explore.

How do we carry out this exploration? How does theology engage the self-understanding of our world so as to bring it into dialogue with the word of God? How can the communities, the systems, and the powers of our society be made aware of the reign of Christ among them? How can we discern the work of the Holy Spirit among the many spirits that possess and move us? The question is, of course, as unbounded as God's creation and as deep as God's covenant promise to all humanity. We can only probe it, not encompass it. Each probe will be at best a faithful witness from one perspective out of one experience, an invitation to enlargement and correction. Nevertheless the task is formidable. To another culture, in another age, the apostle Paul described it:

> To me, though I am the very least of all the saints, this grace was given, to preach to the nations (*ethné*) the unsearchable riches of Christ, and to make all men see what is the economy of the mystery hidden for ages in God who created all things; that through the church the manifold wisdom of God might now be made known to the principalities and powers in the heavenly places (Eph. 3:8–10).

Few of us these days have Paul's combination of humility and chutzpah. Still we—all Christians—are by faith theologians like Paul. So we must try. The reflections that follow in this book are one believer's effort. They are rooted, however, in two communities of faith, thought, and prayer that have shaped, and continue to shape, the author's vision.

The first, and most immediate, is an informal group known on this continent as the Gospel and Our Culture Network. The impetus for it came first from the missionary and ecumenist J. E. Lesslie Newbigin who, in the now well-known story, landed in his native Britain after a lifetime of service in India to discover a secularist pagan land in desperate need of mission itself. In his last years he threw himself into that task, and the movement he founded has crossed the ocean to North America. The conditions on this continent differ in many ways. In an earlier article, I have tried to indicate some of those differences (Hunsberger and van Gelder 1996:214–27). But the challenge is the same. How can we understand and respond in faith to the saving work of God for and in a secularized society with centuries of Christian history behind it? How do we understand the spirits and forces at work in such a society, and relate to its self-understanding? How should theology inform our witness to the reign of Christ and the work of the Spirit there? What should be the form of the church's life and ministry in it?

To these questions the Gospel and Our Culture Network is devoted. Much of what is in these pages has grown out of or has been presented there. The author is grateful to the colleagues of this Network, and to those of a similar project in India in which he was privileged to partake, for encouragement, inspiration, and correction in our common calling.

The other community reaches back further through the years, to the days when a confused student, seeking foundations for his humanistic idealism and undisciplined life, stumbled into the Student Christian Movement. It was the doorway to a new reality—God in Christ as the meaning, the salvation, and the transformation of the world. It was an invitation to join the community that believed that reality, the church ecumenical, in its mission to that world. This student was converted by that gospel and has been a part of that community in various of its forms—the Church of Christ in China, the Evangelical Church in Germany, the World Council of Churches, the Presbyterian Church (U.S.A.), Princeton Theological Seminary, and countless other less formal groups—ever since.

The questions that have driven the ecumenical movement through the twentieth century are the basic ones that confront us today. How is the Triune God at work in the nations and cultures—in the rapid, often brutal, changes and the conflicting powers of the world today? How does the gospel confront our various worldviews? How can we discern the presence of Christ? How can we bear faithful witness to God's word of judgment, redemption, and promise for this world? It should not be surprising, therefore, that this writer may repeat here some themes on which he has previously written in this ecumenical ministry, and may quote again from some sources used before, especially in a book published some thirty years ago, now long out of print, *The Power to Be Human*. It was written in the turbulent sixties when revolution was the crisis of society and Marxism was faith's chief ideological challenge. The world has changed since then, but the gospel still faces many of the same basic issues. Bonhoeffer and Barth still speak to us. So does the perverse prophecy of Karl Marx. So do the words of church leaders and assemblies from those times. My apologies, therefore, to those with long memories who find echoes of the past mixed in the present words here offered. There is method in the repetition.

The chapters that follow explore three fields of Christian witness to the economy of God amid the nations, rulers, and powers in our culture today. They are not the only fields. Others may, from their experience, choose different ones. But they are fields that in one way or another affect us all.

1. What does it mean to say that the gospel is true, not just in the private experience of believers, but for all? How is the truth of God's revelation, known in the response of faith, related to the discernment and validation of truth as it is practiced elsewhere in our culture? How is faith related to the body of knowledge which we discover by other methods and by which we live in the public sphere? Postmodern deconstructionism has helped us in one respect. It has dismantled the public confidence in a universal structure of "objective," "factual" reality known by experimental reason that characterized the humanism of the Enlightenment. But how, then, is any truth claim validated—most especially the claim of the Triune God revealed in Christ—in human minds and hearts? How do we find reliable truth amid conflicting predictions and analyses about the meaning, the purpose, and the destiny of human life?

2. How is the one universal community of the people of God, gathered by the Holy Spirit into the body of

Christ, related to the diverse and competing human communities in which the cultures of the world take form? The biblical message is clear: "Hear, O Israel: the LORD our God is one LORD" (Deut. 6:4). There is no pluralism, there are no divisions, in the One who made the heavens and the earth, who comes to reconcile the world in Jesus Christ by the work of the Holy Spirit. Instead, one community embraces all the variety of nature, all the diversity of humanity in one covenant and one promise of Christ's coming and God's reign. The claim and promise of God for the diverse human and natural world is total. The gospel informs and transforms every culture into which it comes. In and through the body of Christ the cultures of many nations are freed from self-centered fears to flourish as relative historical witnesses to the embracing glory of God. Of this good news we are called to be messengers. Of this community we are members. Of this Lord we are servants.

But it has not always worked this way. The world is plural in its communities, its loyalties, its values and goals, its powers and organizations, and even in the gods it worships. This plurality on the one hand reflects the fullness of God's blessing in creation and history, and on the other hand a field of competing human efforts to organize reality around themselves rather than God. Too often, not least in America, the church through its cultural identifications has been part of this ambiguity. As Christians we are part of the world's pluralism. How then can we discern and embody the gospel so that it points toward the unity of the world in Christ rather than becoming one more of the plural and competing centers of human belief and organization?

3. How is the power of God in the life, death, and resurrection of Jesus Christ related to the human powers at work in the world? The power of God is covenantal. It is expressed in the relationship of justice and mercy, of promise and forgiveness, that God establishes with believers. Christians are stewards of this power, witnesses to the plan of God to fulfill all things in Christ. They are called to deal responsibly with such human power and authority as is given them in the light of this divine work, to make it serve God's covenant in all the variety of its forms.

But powers in this sinful world will never be content with this. They seek always and everywhere to generalize, aggrandize, and absolutize themselves. In the providence of God they do not succeed. In the biblical picture they are expressed through human power, but they also transcend and enslave human beings. Ministry to these powers, through both resistance and witness, calling them to their proper context in the justice of God and the redeeming work of Christ, is a central part of the church's mission. What form does this take among the powers at work in society today, with their various capacities to victimize some and serve the ambitions of others? Who are these powers? How are we to analyze and act toward them so as to bear faithful witness? In what combination of judgment and blessing is God at work among them? To what balance of resistance and legitimization are we called? These are, as theological, also secular questions. Disciplined integrity in discerning the judgment and promise of God on us and our enemies and in seeking secular forms of relative justice is our most effective witness in this sphere to the work of Christ.

# 1

# The Gospel as Truth

---

> Pilate said to him, "So you are a king?" Jesus answered, "You say that I am a king. For this I was born, and for this I have come into the world, to bear witness to the truth. Every one who is of the truth hears my voice." Pilate said to him, "What is truth?" (John 18:37–38a).

Pilate did not expect an answer to his question. He was a governor, not a philosopher. His priorities were authority, law, and order. These he tried to practice as an honest public official of the empire he served. He was surrounded by a welter of competing religious and philosophical truth claims, some of them ready to fight the Roman Empire for their cause or king. Here before him, it appeared, was just one more of these. His job was to maintain imperial power, to execute justice, and to balance the two so as to keep peace in the province assigned to him. These were the pillars of his world. No one knew better than he how precarious they were, how much they depended on the power of Rome and on his skill as an administrator, judge, and diplomat. In this context, it was his responsibility to determine whether this Jesus was a lawbreaker or innocent, a danger to public order or harmless. What could be less relevant to it than the question of "truth"?

All this sounds very contemporary, even postmodern. This may be a hopeful sign. After centuries of imagining that our minds control the truth, the world has come round again to the more honest skepticism of Pilate. But can we build a world on this skepticism? Pilate, to keep the peace as governor, ceremonially washed his hands of the fate of an innocent man and gave him over to death. In that act he paid tribute to a truth that judged him and his world, but with which he could not cope. We too are responsible for our neighbors in this world where truth seems to have no power. We too cannot cope with that responsibility and wash our hands of it in a thousand ways while our fellow human beings suffer. But neither we nor Pilate can escape so easily. What then is this truth that confronts us in Christ, which we find so hard both to live by and to live without?

### Ancient Truth

Already in Jesus' time the word truth had various meanings, drawn from different cultures. The Hebrew word *'emeth* comes from a root that means "to be faithful" or "steadfast." It indicates "a reality that is seen as firm, solid, valid, binding" (Kittel 1932:233). As such it means both the reality itself and the attitude of mind and heart that acknowledges and lives by that reality. It can refer to evidence in a court of law (Deut. 13:4), the correctness of a report, or the reliability of the reporter (Gen. 42:16). *'emeth* applied to persons means trustworthiness (Exod. 18:21), faithfulness (1 Sam. 12:24 et al.), and sincerity (Ps. 15:2; 51:6), all as relations of the human soul to what is real. The objective and the subjective are not separated. They are united in God, who is true. This truth is the power and reign of the One who is steadfast, faithful, and reliable, whose relations with the people of the covenant in the law and in history are just and merciful, judging and delivering. One text must stand for many to make the point:

> Happy is he whose help is the God of Jacob,
>     whose hope is in the LORD his God,
> who made heaven and earth,
>     the sea, and all that is in them;
> who keeps truth [Hebrew: *'emeth*] for ever;
>     who executes justice for the oppressed;
>     who gives food to the hungry.
>
> The LORD sets the prisoners free;
>     the LORD opens the eyes of the blind.
> The LORD lifts up those who are bowed down;
>     the LORD loves the righteous.
> The LORD watches over the sojourners,
>     he upholds the widow and the fatherless;
>     but the way of the wicked he brings to ruin.
> The LORD will reign for ever,
>     thy God, O Zion, to all generations.
> Praise the LORD! (Ps. 146:5–10)

The Greek word for truth, *aletheia*, has a different history. Rooted in the idea of "not hidden," open, or made known, it soon took on the meaning of that which is real in contrast to that which merely seems or appears to be so. Plato made this distinction into a classic dualism that permeated the ancient world. Truth is the changeless form of reality. It is discerned by reason (*logos*) freed from the constraints of passion and material limitations. Whether it took the Stoic form of divine natural law accessible to all rational creatures, or mystical emancipation from the limits of the flesh, the effect was the same. Truth was seen as an eternal order of being beyond the imperfections of this world. History was, in this context, an essentially meaningless process of creation and decay. The covenant relationships—faithfulness, righteousness, promise, grace, and love—in which truth, for the Hebrews, was embodied, were subordinated to changeless perfection. For many Hellenistic Jews who tried to reconcile the two worldviews, God was identified with eternal order. Revelation became enlightenment. Evil was identified with the flesh, and salvation became liberation from it into an eternal realm of true light and pure reason.

The New Testament directs both of these streams into one focus—the truth of God in the incarnation, crucifixion, and resurrection of Jesus Christ. Greek dualism lurks in the background. How could it not, when it permeated the culture everywhere? The letters to Ephesians and Colossians especially confront the cosmology of the Hellenic world with the creation, redemption, and fulfillment of all things in Christ. But it is the Gospel of John that presents the challenge most directly: "The Word (*logos*) became (*egeneto*) flesh (*sarx*) and dwelt among us, full of grace and truth (*aletheia*)" (1:14a). John uses the ideas of Greek philosophy—*logos, egeneto, sarx,* and *aletheia*—to tear them out of their timeless, dualistic worldview and make them descriptions of God at work through Christ in the creation, history, and promise of this human and material world. Truth is in the incarnate Christ, who is also the way and the life (14:6). If we continue in his *logos* we will know the truth (*aletheia*) that sets us free (8:31–32). He was in the beginning with God and was God. Through him all things were made (*egeneto*). In him was life, which was the light of men (1:1–4). His work will continue in the Spirit of truth, which will make known to believers the things that are to come (16:13).

All of this makes one fundamental point: Truth is in the triune God who created this world, who came into it in Jesus Christ, and who in the Holy Spirit guides us toward the fulfillment of all things in Christ. This is ultimate reality. Human ideas about the structure of the true and the good are episodes in the drama of this relationship.

More dramatic than this disentanglement of faith from Hellenic culture, however, is the New Testament conflict with some Jews and Judaizers over the truth claim of Christ. Jesus was rough: "If I tell the truth, why do you not believe me? [Whoever] is of God hears the words of God; the reason why you do not hear them is that you are not of God" (John 8:46–47). The Pharisees who questioned him believed that the truth of God was embodied in the calling and the covenant of their ancestry, which formed their nation: "We are descendants of Abraham" (8:32). Jesus confronted them with a new form of that covenant, which reaffirmed the old but broke its bondage to ethnicity. The truth of God may be revealed to a people, "salvation is from the Jews" (4:22b), but it is not *in* their culture or their ancestry. "The hour is coming, and now is, when the true worshipers will worship the Father in spirit and truth" (4:23a).

Nor is the truth of God in the law, though the law may both express it and obscure it. "For the wrath of God is revealed from heaven against all impiety and unrighteousness of men who hold the truth captive in unrighteousness," writes Paul to the Romans, "for what can be known of God is plain to them, because God has shown it to them" (1:18–19, my trans. from the Greek). Because therefore, "they exchanged the truth about God for a lie and worshiped and served the creature rather than the Creator" (1:25). The judgment of God falls according to truth on those who do such things (2:2). They know the truth, and in their unrighteousness are false to it.

Yet they are not *in* the truth. They know of God but do not know God. This is what makes the legal truth they do know either a lie or a condemnation. Human sin can and does continually distort knowledge, even true knowledge about reality, even about the reality of God. Missing is a living relationship with the God of the covenant whose power and promise the prophets and the psalms proclaimed and who has come on earth in Jesus Christ. Excluded is the truth of the gospel (Gal. 2:5), the good news that we are justified not by our own goodness but solely and completely by God's forgiving and sanctifying grace, expressed in Christ's calling, teaching, death, resurrection, presence in the church, and coming reign in the world. Truths that are generated from the center of our human selves—truths of reason, law, and culture—are relative, partial, and often corrupted by their source. When they claim too much for themselves, they become instruments of human power against other humans. When they justify the behavior of the powerful, they become lies. Christ the truth invites us into a relationship wherein we die to self and find ourselves in the context of a new reality whose mystery we explore without ever being ourselves in control. "From now on, therefore, we regard no one from a human point of view; even though we once knew Christ from a human point of view, we know him no longer in that way. Therefore, if any one is in Christ, there is a new creation; the old has passed away, see the new has come. All this is from God, who reconciled us to himself through Christ and has given us the ministry of reconciliation" (2 Cor. 5:16–18 NRSV).

We find ourselves, therefore, in a truth that we do not control but that liberates and calls us as children of God. Truth is, in the New Testament, the certainty of faith, the relation of trust with the God who claims us and our world in Christ. It is expressed (1) in free response to that claim and that ministry by reflecting the justice, the forgiving grace, the faithful love, and the redeeming promise of God in Christ; (2) in our own relations with other people and with God; and (3) in our witness to its saving truth for an unbelieving world.

This biblical heritage projects a fourfold insight into human knowledge in the world where human creatures in every age are called to live.

First, truth is whole, and we who seek it are part of the wholeness we perceive. Cosmology and ethics, creation and humanity, belong together, and the truth about one cannot be separated from the truth about the other. Human beings are participants in it all, while they are also observers. We confess and live by it while we are investigating it. Verification must be sought not only in the coherence of a rational structure but also in true guidance for human life.

On this, to be sure, the whole ancient world agreed. The religions of Babylon and Egypt combined the heavens and the earth, the power of the gods and the power of the ruler, in one mythological order that embraced nature and humanity. The philosophers of Greece and Rome subordinated myth to reason, but the reason in which they believed was a perceiving point within, not outside of, the ordered universe it described. The truth discovered placed the philosopher himself in its harmony and prescribed his form of life.

The biblical witness differed not in its view of the wholeness of truth, but in the way in which that wholeness is made known and acknowledged by human beings. Not cosmological order, perceived by myth or by reason, not some human vision that embraced the gods, the powers of nature, and human society, but the revelation of God, made known in word and act toward a particular people, leads them into the wholeness of truth. Cosmology is present in images borrowed from Babylonian myths, but it is transformed to tell quite a different story—of the work of the Creator who is first of all the God of the calling, the promise, and the covenant. The image of God in human beings is not in some human capacity such as reason, but in the whole response of the believers to the One who calls them into being, community, and history. Truth is whole—as whole as the mystery of the trinitarian depths of the creating, redeeming, and sanctifying purpose of God.

Second, truth is the quality of a living relationship, not a structure of being, not the text of a statement, whether of doctrine or law. Objectively, it is the self-revelation of the triune God coming to men and women created for one another in God's image and played out (1) in the biblical struggle with a believing but disobedient people, and ultimately (2) in Christ's life, crucifixion, and resurrection. Subjectively, it is known by faith responding to God with the whole self and using the mind to explore both creation and human life in the light of God's covenant, gift, and promise.

Here, agreement has not been nearly so unanimous, even among believers. "We preach Christ crucified," said Paul defiantly, "a stumbling block to Jews and foolishness to Gentiles, but to those who are called, both Jews and Greeks, Christ the power of God and the wisdom of God" (1 Cor. 1:23–24 NRSV). To understand truth this way means to surrender the security of absolute knowledge. It demands the risk of personal commitment to the God whom one trusts but whose mind one can never fully understand. It means, as Dietrich Bonhoeffer put it years ago (1978:30–37), to ask first not the question, what? or how?, but the central question, who? Who are you, who calls us, who claims us in our whole being, who surrounds us with this covenant and this love, who leads us through death to new creation and promises the fulfillment of all things in you? The search for truth is conducted in the second person, in prayerful reflection, in the obedience of faith, not in third-person analyses and conclusions.

Even Christians have found this hard to live with. Fear of relativism on the one hand and subjectivism on the other have plagued the church through the centuries. The controversies of the fourth century were a desperate attempt to capture in creeds the living mystery of

Christ's divine and human nature. They resulted in stating paradoxes which precisely as such have become part of the church's confession. The churches of the Reformation broke fellowship with one another over defining the manner of Christ's presence in the eucharist. It has taken more than four centuries to heal the breach. The Roman Catholic Church sharpened its doctrine of papal infallibility as late as the nineteenth century to protect its magisterium, and finds itself ever since in inner controversy over the nature of that authority. Truth cannot be captured. Doctrines are helpful only as guides in our commitment to the One who reveals truth step-by-step in relation to us. There is no faith without the risk of error that responsible witness brings. God alone is the lord of truth. We by faith may be its servants.

Third, truth becomes falsehood when it is no longer true to the relationship with God that it claims to express. Human beings are always trying to capture truth for themselves and for the powers they serve. It may be the power of reason in a philosophy, the power of tradition in the religion and customs of a people, the power of rulers in government and law, the power of economic prosperity and success, or the power of a revolutionary dream. All people do so, even believers who think that they are thereby serving God. But truth, when it is so captured, becomes the instrument of conflict and destruction. Christian truthfulness lies in continual witness to the One who judges, corrects, and transforms all human claims, even our own, to know and possess the truth of God.

Fourth, truth is historical, as we are and as God has chosen to be. It comes to us in events in which God is at work. It comes in the living word of judgment and redeeming grace that interacts with the history of human religions, cultures, and civilizations with all their conflicts, based on what happened in the history of the Jews and in the coming of Christ. This is known as a scandal to cosmopolitan spirits—the scandal of particularity. That God's truth should take the form of a cosmic myth or a general principle such as holiness, goodness, or love would be worthy of universal divinity. But to choose an obscure people in the hills east of the Mediterranean Sea, to covenant with them, judge, guide, save them, and make them witnesses to God's truth in the obedience and disobedience of their historical acts—this violates all normal concepts of how Deity should behave. Add then that God became human as a Palestinian Jew, that he belonged to that nation, that he entered into its religion, its culture, and its politics with good news of his coming reign, that he died on the cross at the hands of the Romans and rejected by his people, that he rose from the dead and from this base sent forth his apostles with a gospel of salvation for all the nations of the world—and almost nothing seems to be left of cosmic transcendent truth.

Yet God did so act. Truth is not found outside history but in it, in the concrete ways God deals with us in its particular events. It is this God who created the heavens and the earth as the first historical act and who embraces all nature and humanity in the drama which began with Israel, reached its climax in the coming of Christ, and is being played out in the mission of the church to all the cultures and peoples of the world. Truth about our lives and society in each time emerges from careful attention to the God whom the biblical history reveals and who is at work among us now and until the end of the age.

## Modern Truth

Humanity has lived with these insights now for nearly two thousand years. We have still not learned to live *by* them. In a thousand ways we continually try to escape the limits of the relationship within which knowledge is true. We try to become ourselves masters of truth. In Western Euro-American society, which tradition has called Christendom, the seeds were already sown in the controversies over doctrine and church authority mentioned above. They bore fruit, however, in what seemed the emancipation of human minds from the arbitrary control of these very dogmas and persons. God's truth in the late Middle Ages had itself become for many a system, a synthesis, of biblical story with Stoic law and Aristotelian cosmology. It was enforced by a human magisterium that resisted insights that threatened its structure or authority. Where could the early modern scientist find a context for the new facts he was discovering or the new theories that gave them meaning?

These scientists were themselves believing Christians. Galileo, the great example of this controversy, set the truth of his observation-based theory about the movement of the earth and the sun against the cosmology of the Middle Ages, but he did so as a pious Christian who finally yielded to the authority of the church. Johannes Kepler, exploring and explaining the movements of the stars, felt that he was "thinking God's thoughts after him." René Descartes based his confidence that the clear and distinct ideas in his mind are true, on the argument that God, who is "altogether perfect and trustworthy," was the source both of the ideas and of the realities to which they corresponded (1958:123–25. Discourse on Method, Pt. IV). Such men, and others like them, knew the character of the Triune God in the teaching and sacraments of the church. They trusted this redeeming and sanctifying God as creator of all things and were empowered by that trust to explore creation using the methods of empirical science. In the words of an English philosopher, "The modern investigators of nature were the first to take seriously *in their science* the Christian doctrine that nature is created, and the main difference between the methods of ancient and the methods of modern natural science may be reduced to this: that these are and those are not methods proper to the investigation of a created nature" (Foster 1934:446–48).

The consequences of this liberation have been incalculable. Freed from final and formal causes to explore nature as a created, and therefore contingent, secular reality, science has discovered millions of new connections and relationships among natural phenomena and has given them structure in ever-changing theories. The one condition that authorized both scientific knowledge and technological development is that they *be* empirical and practical, concerned with the created phenomena of nature in relation to human life, that the reality they discover and create *be* secular and contingent with relation to the Creator, and that they find meaning and direction as part of the human drama whose center is Jesus Christ.

But this was not, as we know, the direction that science and technology took. Instead, the Christian church had to orient itself to a quite different drama—

scientists borrowing the concept of "God" as a working hypothesis to hold secular systems of thought and action together while they pursued their investigations and their inventions. This was followed by a rejection of this God in favor of a critical but basic confidence in the empirical scientific method itself to discover all truth, and in technological progress to produce the human future. For example:

1. Already in the twelfth century, Canon Hugh of the Abbey of St. Victor found human technological enterprise to be authorized in God's command to Adam and Eve to "fill the earth and subdue it" and have dominion "over every living thing" (Gen. 1:28). This authorization, reinstated for humanity in Christ's restoration of the image of God, meant that technology was a blessed activity, looking toward the fulfillment of all things in Christ's reign. Five centuries later, Francis Bacon carried the idea into the modern age. In the Fall, he wrote, both dominion over nature and the knowledge of nature were lost, along with the image of God. But today, after the coming of Christ, humans are called to recover that image by scientific investigation of nature and control over it. Thus they will restore the relation to God that they had lost. Bacon here is still a believer. The hope of communion with God is the motivation for technological progress. But his God is already captive to the scientific and technological enterprise itself.

2. A century later such a God was no longer necessary. Adam Smith put his faith in the moral sentiments of human nature itself (Smith 1976), which, though

perhaps related to God, did not need God to explain their origin or their function in the world. On this faith he built the system of free enterprise and market economy that dominates the world today. The natural ambitions of individuals seeking their own best interest and greatest gain would weave into the marketplace a system of production and exchange that itself would take the place of God in creating social harmony and promoting human progress as long as time endures (Smith 1978).

3. In natural science, for Descartes, God is indeed a working hypothesis, necessary to guarantee that our perceptions correspond to reality. But this Deity is pure thinking substance, defined by the function given it. It may be identified with the God of Christian revelation—and indeed Descartes did so—but it is not, in itself, this God. Isaac Newton, who followed Descartes a century later, was a theologian as well as a scientist. He firmly believed that there were two levels of discourse—the mechanical and the religious. He rejoiced that there were mysteries in the natural world—he named specifically the orbits of the planets in a firmament of fixed stars and the biological mechanism of the eye—that science could not explain and that must therefore be referred to the providence of God.

But as science expanded the limits of its discoveries, these mysteries gave way more and more to "mechanical" explanation. The French astronomer Laplace at the turn of the nineteenth century firmly closed the gap. He presupposed the principles of Newtonian mechanics: that a complete system of natural laws determines the behavior of material things and can be discovered by experimental science. He dismissed the question of origins, and therefore of history, as meaningless. On this basis he projected the universe as a self-sufficient rational system that could, theoretically, be understood in the totality of its laws and operations by a mind sufficiently endowed with mathematical ability and knowledge of all the conditions in a given moment of time. There is no such mind, of course, he believed; but the universe so functioned. The story is told that when the Emperor Napoleon asked him where God was in his system, he replied, "Sire, I haven't needed that hypothesis."

Thus was born—and one could multiply the illustrations—the modern humanist worldview that has dominated Western society during most of the past two centuries. Lesslie Newbigin, in his now famous polemic, calls it a pagan culture, "born out of the rejection of Christianity" (1986:20). David Bosch, both in his massive *Transforming Mission* (1986:264ff) and in his posthumous essay *Believing in the Future* (1995:5), supports this view. Their composite picture of this humanist culture provides a good summary:

a. It is a culture in which human reason is the source of all knowledge. This reason proceeds by the empirical method, moving from experimental observation under controlled conditions to generalizations about the object, which are called laws and are subject to verification or falsification by further experiment. Thus the order of nature is discovered by the procedures of the human mind. There can be no revelation.

b. It is based on a sharp separation between subject and object. Knowledge is about objective facts. The subject's relation to it is only that of an empirical investigator. Nature, including human nature, is an object to be investigated. Truth is not awareness of reality to be explored and responded to in mutual relationships. It is factual information about the object that enables the thinking subject to understand its workings and therefore to control and use it.

c. It is a culture in which all reference to purpose or goal is relegated to subjective opinion. There are no formal or final causes in the nature of things. Truth deals only with efficient causes, with how things work, with predictability as established by repeated experimental establishment of cause and effect.

d. It is a culture in which knowledge is essentially ahistorical. Newbigin quotes the German philosopher Lessing's dictum: "The accidental truths of history can never establish universal truths of reason" (1989:2). What is unique and nonrepeatable is by definition meaningless. The structure and processes of nature are governed by timeless laws.

Yet this same culture believes almost axiomatically in the endless cumulative progress of human knowledge and in the power it brings. Images of discovery, invention, expanding economy, transformation of human life, and light out of darkness express its hope. Development and modernization are its key words.

e. It is a culture that believes that objective facts are true and that values are a matter of subjective opinion. Factual knowledge is that which stands on its own, regardless of the perspective or belief of the knowing subject. Search for this objectivity is built into the empirical method. This method is built on doubt, questioning everything that seems to be true or that the investigator for any reason would like to accept as true, until evidence independent of all desire or point of view establishes a truth as "fact." It follows that religious beliefs and values are private, emotive expressions, matters of personal preference. They can be left to free choice in a field of unlimited pluralism, because they are not relevant to factual reality.

f.   It is a culture that believes all problems are solvable, given the knowledge of relevant facts and their application. More and more, the world of nature can be controlled and planned for human purposes and according to human designs. There is no mystery at the heart of things. God, if he or she exists, is in the human planning reason, or just ahead of it, inspiring and confirming its goals.

g.   It is a culture built on the self-expression of free autonomous individuals, pursuing their own goals. Freedom means free choice, free enterprise, the free pursuit of one's own happiness. Authority therefore is inherently suspect, whether it comes from government, from God or the church, or even from teachers or parents. Cultivation of free self-determination, in voluntary but never mandatory cooperation with others, should take its place.

Both Bosch and Newbigin recognize that this Enlightenment culture has produced enormous benefits for humanity, many of which should be theologically justified and supported. Political liberty, democracy, social tolerance, human rights, the critical questioning and renewal of tradition, practical optimism about solving human problems, and active, hopeful participation in the vast development of human powers and more creative lifestyles, are among them. We cannot go back on any of these achievements. Indeed, we should recognize that they are to a great extent a humanist effort to realize the promise of God in Christ reconciling the world to himself. At the same time, they are a revolt against a Christianity that had encapsulated this promise in a dualistic worldview and a conservative church.

Nevertheless, this culture rested on what Bosch calls two inconsistent plausibility structures (1995:17), one biblical-Christian and practiced in the church, the other humanist, mechanistic, and practiced in the world of work and public life. This pattern goes back well into the seventeenth century. It produced an ongoing Christian apologetic, along with continual efforts at reconciling the two. In fact, however, these efforts too often led to the gradual surrender of Christian faith to Enlightenment humanist premises. For example, consider the following:

*The redefinition of Christian faith as a religion, in the effort to defend it as true religion.* John Calvin could not have foreseen the consequences when he titled his major work *The Institutes of the Christian Religion.* He used the term *religio* only occasionally and clearly in the sense that previous centuries had understood—the general form or discipline that expresses reverence for God. "Here, indeed, is pure and real religion," he wrote, defining it, "Faith so joined with an earnest fear of God, that this fear also embraces willing reverence, and carries with it such legitimate worship as is prescribed in the law" (1961:43, Bk. I, Chap. ii, 2).

Later generations of Reformed and Lutheran theologians, however, gradually changed this definition. They were earnest apologists, concerned to defend revealed, scriptural, orthodox truth against the rising tide of Cartesian philosophy. But in doing so they adopted, step-by-step, their opponents' understanding of truth and of the methods for discerning it. First, religion was defined as a neutral phenomenon embracing doctrine and practice, in order to prove that Christian faith is the true religion, the only one that meets the standards of the definition. Then the idea of natural religion was developed, a general human awareness of the nature and commands of God, to be supplemented by revelation, but also to be used to demonstrate the adequacy of Christian revelation to religious truth. Calvin's definition of religion was turned from a statement about human response to God into a statement about human beliefs concerning God. Faithful versus unfaithful gave place to true versus false. True religion became right doctrine, known by the mind as an object, logically prior to the engagement of the whole self with the One who reveals and claims. From there it was only one step to try to demonstrate that Christianity was the "true religion" by reaching for arguments that would convince those outside the community of response to God's own word and calling. Christian faith took its place as one account among others of the phenomenon, religion (cf. Barth 1956:Par. 17).

*The location of faith primarily in human religious experience, which becomes the assurance and guarantor for the truth of that which is experienced.* Of course, neither the Moravian pietists of eighteenth-century Germany nor the revivalists of nineteenth-century America intended to consign the gospel to a purely subjective realm. Nor did Friedrich Schleiermacher, the great theologian of human religion. Rather, they were concerned to affirm the integrity of human feeling, intuition, and experience as themselves a way, beyond the "objectifying consciousness" of bourgeois science, by which reality, above all the reality of God, may be known. Religion "wishes to intuit the universe, wishes devoutly to overhear the universe's own manifestations and actions" (Schleiermacher 1988:22).

What they actually achieved, however, was a double surrender to the worldview they opposed. First, they brought the individualism of the Enlightenment into the sphere of faith; second, they introduced another human standard for knowing and testing the truth of revelation. Not the rational subject, but the experiencing subject became the arbiter. The "religious affections" (Schleiermacher) reached out for God, and Christian doctrines were commended as the most complete response to those affections. God's revelation, the meaning and destiny of human life in history, was validated by its satisfaction of human emotions. The words of a familiar revival hymn come to mind: "He lives! He lives! Salvation to impart. You ask me how I know he lives; he lives within my heart!"

Such an understanding of the truth of the gospel, Lesslie Newbigin rightly observes, "could, perhaps, at least until the arrival of modern psychology, provide a hiding place for religion from the searing light of science, a space within the modern world for the continued cultivation of an archaic form of self-consciousness. But it could not challenge the ideology that ruled the public world" (1986:45). Indeed, it became part—the religious part—of that world.

*The attempt by some conservatives to turn theology itself into a science, using the assumptions and methods of modern scientific rationalism to explore, expound, and defend the truths of the Bible.* The nineteenth-century Princeton theologian Charles Hodge puts the case forcefully and clearly:

> It is the fundamental principle of all sciences, and of theology among the rest, that theory is to be determined by facts, and not facts by theory. As natural science was a chaos until the principle of induction was admitted and faithfully carried out, so theology is a jumble of human speculations, not worth a straw, when men refuse to apply the same principle to the Word of God. The true method of theology is, therefore, the inductive, which assumes that the Bible contains all the facts or truths which form the contents of theology, just as the facts of nature are the contents of the natural sciences. It is also assumed that the relation of these Biblical facts to each other, the principles involved in them, the laws which determine them, are in the facts themselves and are to be deduced from them, just as the laws of nature are deduced from the facts of nature (Hodge 1981:14–15, 17; cf. Stewart 1998:26–28).

There is an ingenious irony in this proposal. Charles Hodge has a point. If science assumes a field of facts about nature as its basic reality, why should not theology make the same assumption concerning the facts in the Bible about God? Are not both, in their ways, revelations waiting to be interpreted? If the method of scientific investigation is empirical and inductive, strictly controlled by the object, why should not theology be similarly inductive and controlled in its study of the biblical text? Is not this method the way to objective truth in both cases? To be sure, Hodge recognizes: "The truths of religion are far more important than those of natural science. They come home to the heart and the conscience." But for this very reason the theologian must be more on guard than the scientist against subjective bias, "more diligent and faithful in collecting the facts which (God) has made known and giving them their due weight" (1981:12).

One could almost imagine that Hodge was writing a parody on the pretensions of humanist science. But he was no satirist; he was serious, as his successors are today. The Bible contains all the factual truths about God and humanity. But the Bible is words. This leads inevitably to some doctrine of verbal inspiration that guarantees its truth. It also makes the Bible itself ultimate. God the revealer recedes behind the revealed text. The relation of the believer is to stories and statements from which truth is deduced. This believer then becomes, as a rational self, the knower and the arbiter of the truth of God, grasping it rather than being grasped by it. Factual knowledge comes first; worship and obedience may follow, but as consequent choices, not as part of the knowing act itself. Assent to certain doctrines, presumed to be fundamental and derived logically from biblical texts, becomes the test of faith.

In short, this effort to build an impregnable fortress for Christian truth against the humanist culture of the day, using the materials and methods of that culture itself, has produced a tower of Babel. Its builders are autonomous human subjects. Its materials are objective "facts." Its methods are rational grasp and control of these facts. Although much genuine piety and faithful obedience to the word of the living God is present in this fortress (how could it be otherwise when that word is still present and heard?), the structure itself is a humanist enterprise that depends on its enemies for its foundations and its architecture.

## Postmodern Truth

So modern culture in the Euro-American world faces a double breakdown. On the one hand, though the gospel of transforming judgment and grace is still proclaimed, the structure of Christian response to the biblically revealed and living God has been weakened and undermined by a thousand gradual surrenders to the humanist premises of the Enlightenment worldview. We have reviewed above only a few of the most coherent. On the other hand, the Enlightenment worldview itself has continually drawn on the spiritual resources of a Christian tradition in which its proponents still live, though they have tried to relegate this tradition to the private, subjective realm. When these resources run out, we face what, for lack of positive signs, we call a postmodern world with a new approach to truth, a new culture, and a new challenge to the mission of the church. This has happened, I suggest, in three stages.

The first of these started already in the eighteenth century. Doubt was cast on the capacity of the human mind, using experimental scientific methods, to obtain

accurate knowledge of external reality. The epistemological problem raised by Descartes—how can we be
sure that the ideas in our mind correspond to facts in
nature?—continued to plague philosophy and science
until it met its nemesis in David Hume and Immanuel
Kant. Hume was a fundamental skeptic. There is no
way, he maintained, in which the necessary connections of ideas in our mind can be rationally shown to
reflect the structure of the world outside. Reason can
say nothing about existence; it can speak only of the
internal consistency of thoughts. No comparison of
ideas can ever prove facts in the existing world to be or
not to be the case. All inferences from experience,
therefore, are effects of custom, not of reasoning
(1967:Bk. I). So it is also in ethics. Reason can
describe the relation of means to ends, but it can never
decide between right and wrong in the choice of ends.
Hume did believe finally in humanity, but his confidence lay in the customs and conventions of the
human mind and society, with the natural sympathy
and "moral passions" they expressed (Bk. II).

Kant was a still more rigorous critic, and yet a more
confident defender of the Enlightenment enterprise.
The human mind cannot know things in themselves,
but only phenomena that are experienced and intuited.
Pure reason organizes these phenomena into rational
categories and causal connections. It generalizes them
into scientific laws. But there is no way we can prove
a correspondence between these categories and things
in themselves. Our rational knowledge is a contribu-
tion of the human mind to natural reality, not a reflection of it. In a similar way, Kant refutes the traditional

arguments for the existence of God. They are rationally consistent, but only in the mind; they cannot prove that the rational idea exists (1938:525ff).

Nevertheless, Kant was supremely confident in the benevolent power of human reason. "Dare to know!" he urged in a passionate essay, *What Is Enlightenment?* "Have courage to use your own understanding! This is the slogan of the Enlightenment" (1964:74; my trans.). The world can be grasped by the critical but active use of organizing reason by free, mature persons. It can be shaped for good, because the pure reason as practical—not in ideas but in awareness of duty, not in the indicative but the imperative mood—can express true reality in action through the formal instrument of the goodwill. The moral law is within. It is known not in conditional propositions but directly as goodwill in action. God, rejected in theory, is known as, in Kant's words, a postulate of the practical reason. "Enlightenment was, for Kant, the unconditional, boundless, and therefore finally uncertain self-affirmation of Reason" (Barth 1973:272).

With this self-confidence and this uncertainty, Enlightenment humanism has molded and unsettled society down to our present age. Its successes in scientific discovery and technological progress have been overwhelming. Who can question the truthfulness of knowledge that has harnessed the energy of nature to multiply the power and prosperity of human life, conquered diseases, and united the world with transport and telecommunications? Who cares about other truth that is not useful and that we do not control?

Still doubts arose already in the nineteenth century, and they are still with us. Adam Smith believed that

the science of economics in free market economy discovered laws that would work naturally toward justice,
liberty, and prosperity. His nineteenth-century successors Thomas Malthus and David Ricardo developed the
science but came to different conclusions about its
benevolence. Malthus linked prosperity to population
growth, to demonstrate that the standard of living for
most workers could neither rise far above subsistence
levels because well-being would cause population to rise
and wages to fall, nor fall far below subsistence, because
people would starve. Ricardo discerned an inevitable
conflict in the distribution of production between land-
lords, capitalists, and workers. One group could prosper
only at the cost of the others. It was he, not Karl Marx,
who first discovered class war. Not for nothing was economics in that age labeled the dismal science.

Nor was the benevolence of scientific truth questioned only by economists. Charles Darwin's discovery
of the evolution of species by natural selection was in
itself only a biological theory. The philosopher Herbert
Spencer, however, had no trouble seeing its implications for human society. It is wrong, it is counterproductive, he believed, to interfere with the process by
which some people survive and others perish in the
economic competition of life. The law of nature itself
perfects the species by eliminating its unfit; private
compassion for the victims and government regulation
for the common good are both misplaced introductions
of moral concerns into a natural process.

Is scientific truth then cold and inhuman? Is it
indifferent to all moral values and to all human love
and justice? Is it really truth, or is it only such knowledge as the human mind constructs as it experiments

with and controls natural phenomena? Can humanity use the scientific truth it discovers to destroy both itself and its environment? If not, how are scientific truth and moral truth related? Such underlying questions have plagued the scientific humanist worldview from the beginning. The splitting of the atom and the explosion of technology in our century, with all their consequences, have only made them more urgent.

The second stage began already in the nineteenth century, and intensified in the twentieth, when the truth claims of scientific humanism faced a deeper challenge. It came from within, from prophets who were on the whole explicit atheists, but who brought critical insights to bear that were drawn from Christian theology. Sigmund Freud revealed the non-rational, self-absorbed depths of the human psyche. Friedrich Nietzsche explored the heights and tragic depths of the human will to power. Twentieth-century existentialists like Jean Paul Sartre and Albert Camus dramatized the consequences of ambiguous human motivations in a world where people have no point of reference beyond themselves. But by far the most influential of them was Karl Marx.

Marx was a militant humanist and, therefore, an atheist. "Philosophy does not conceal it," he wrote as a young man in his doctoral dissertation. "The confession of Prometheus, 'in one round sentence, I hate all the gods' is its own confession against all the gods in heaven and on earth who do not acknowledge the human self-consciousness as the highest deity. No other may stand beside him" (1964:15). Humanity, he believed, created itself by its own work, mastering and constructing the objective world. The human species universalizes itself by its action. Kant's problem with the phenomenal character of knowledge and his solution in moral awareness are both irrelevant. The human being *produces* truth, by working on objective reality, to make it reflect a human purpose (1978:75–76).

At the same time, Marx's basic experience of human existence is alienation from this true humanity. It has come about, he believed, because some have appropriated the labor—the very selfhood—of others in the form of private property. Thus arises class conflict, the basic fact of history as we know it, and the determinant of all human thought and action. "It is not the human consciousness that determines human existence," he wrote. "On the contrary, their social existence determines their consciousness" (1978:4). There is no truth, there is no morality, above the class conflict. Knowledge itself is a tool of the social struggle. The very claim to universal validity is itself a weapon in that struggle. Only in a classless society, where all things are held in common after the revolution, will human conflict disappear and universal truth finally emerge. Until then all truth is ideological, that is, the instrument of the self-interest of one social class against another. Religion—by which Marx meant Judaism and Christianity because he knew no other—is a special case, but it is no exception. It is the illusory reality in which the proletarians drown the pain of the inhuman reality in which they live; it is the means by which the exploiting classes justify their dominance and sedate the proletariat with imaginary hopes and satisfactions.

This Marxist challenge has sunk deep into the consciousness of the twentieth-century world. A whole discipline of the sociology of knowledge has arisen to explore the ways in which social position, experience, and community affect the self-understanding of various groups. Cultures and religions have learned to question one another and themselves in new ways. A "hermeneutic of suspicion" has arisen in both religious and secular thought that analyzes economic, political, and social truth claims in the light of the groups in society whose interests they serve. Marxist philosophers, movements, and governments themselves have been subjected to such critical analysis from within and from without. Everywhere in the world today, the question of ideological bias pervades political, economic, cultural, and even scientific-technological debate. How can people, governments, corporations, and societies, thinking from conflicting loyalties, interests, and experiences, discover the truth about what is actually happening to the natural environment? About what will be the economic consequences of world trade agreements? About how safe nuclear power production is or can be made? Ideologies clash on these and countless other issues in the media every day. Thanks to Marx, we can recognize them as such.

Thus, the internal doubts and perplexities of the humanist modern worldview, with too little participation by theology and the witness of the church, have pointed the way into the third stage, postmodernity itself.

The problem is that our very questioning describes our lostness. We know what we can no longer trust and believe; we have not found an alternative. Indeed, many who express this mood would discourage us from looking, for there is nothing to be found. Postmodernism is clearly loss of confidence in the

Enlightenment humanist worldview and the empirical scientific method for discovering truth—but not in the name of some other truth claim, and certainly not that of the Christian gospel. We are awash in relativism. We celebrate pluralism and free self-expression, but we are without common direction and vaguely anxious about our future. To make things worse, we are in the midst of a world of many cultures which we no longer dominate, which confront us with their worldviews and their truth claims.

Postmodernity, then, is a condition in which late twentieth-century culture finds itself. We are all in it, whether Christians or secularists or other believers, even though we may not like it or accept its expressions in philosophy, technology, economics, the media, or the arts. How can we understand it? How can we discern God's truth in and for it? In response to this vast question, let me offer three brief excursions into the landscape.

First, nuclear physics was the first area of modern science to lose confidence in the objectivity of the truth that its methods discovered. It began when Albert Einstein undermined the mechanical model of nature with his theory of relativity. It continued when Niels Bohr and Werner Heisenberg developed the complementarity of two contradictory concepts of light: as wave and as quantum. "No sharp distinction can be made between the behavior of the objects themselves and their interaction with the measuring instruments," wrote Bohr (1958:61). Truth is therefore a statement, a theory, about the relation between the subject and object of an experiment, and contradictory theories may be fruitful to further discovery. Einstein could not accept this, but, as Michael Polanyi has pointed out, Einstein himself is a prime example of changing the vision of true reality in physics by contributing his own creative theory that placed all the facts in a new context (1964:144). Truth, as these physicists have discovered, is, even in science, not objective but relational. Verification is finally not by experiment alone, but by communal acceptance of the meaningfulness of the theory.

But the forces of change could not stay in the realm of theory. Nuclear physics was at stake; the issue was power. "The scientific law," the German physicist-philosopher Carl Friedrich von Weizsäcker pointed out, "becomes more and more only an indication in regard to the possibility and result of experiments; a law concerning our ability to produce phenomena" (1952:200). How far was nuclear research discovering truth about the physical object, the atom and its components, and how far was it imposing on the atom such human concepts as would enable us to control its forces for human ends? How can one distinguish these two objectives, and what is the truth about physics, if any, that embraces them both? To state it bluntly, is knowledge about nuclear fission that can result in the destruction of large parts of the world in any meaningful sense truth? There is no doubt about the power, the functionality, and the usefulness of this knowledge, but does it grasp reality? Is there a meaningful reality out there to be grasped? Von Weizsäcker puts the question eloquently:

> Does the world mean nothing? Is only that person happy—if such a one there be—who can forever evade the question of the meaning and the right with which he uses his knowledge and his

power? Does nothing remain for the others who have run through the movement of modern times but that, in addition to the two ancient aspects of the world: suffering and guilt, meaninglessness has entered as a third?... I do not believe it. I do believe, however, that we must first see the abyss, must bear the emptiness. But I believe that this emptiness means, not the end, but the demand for a decision. Does God no longer speak to us? Our substitute symbolism has broken down not because it was symbolism but because it was a substitute. But the silence which has taken its place is eloquent enough. We must in fact know only whether we want to hear God at all—not where we wish to hear him but where he really speaks to us (1952:277–78).

There is an emptiness in the world of physical science today. It is the emptiness of enormous power that has discovered no guidance, no real meaning, in the object it investigates and the truths it discovers. At best it has established a relationship with that object which may be esthetically satisfying in theory but still reflects the perspective of the human mind producing the realities it discovers. At the same time, it is caught up in human forces, which it magnifies technologically a thousand times, that themselves have no clear sense of direction. Modified as this may be by the many useful and humane uses to which physical discoveries have been put, the question remains, How and where does God speak into this world a truth that is not a human product?

Second, not long ago the world was locked in a conflict between two massive systems of theory and practice—

one capitalist, one communist—each proclaiming itself
as the truth of human society. Both were humanist, in
that the human subject was the source of all knowledge,
and the self-development of the human being through
science, technology, production of goods, and the mas-
tery of nature was the goal of life. Each denounced the
falsehood of the other, and each regarded the conflict
as fundamental. Yet in their competition, they modified each other. Marx and the socialist movement
drove home to the capitalist free enterprise system that
its economic science and laws were a form of false consciousness rooted in the self-interest of the exploiting
class. It was Marxist socialism that projected the vision
of a society in which private profit would give way to
the common good, where poverty would be abolished
along with wealth, and where conflict based on greed
would be suppressed. These were postmodern insights;
they were also grounded in pre-modern Christian
insights into the character of human sin and the nature
of social justice. They forced a liberal humanist world to
take seriously the ideological influence of private economic power in defining the common good and controlling public policy. They induced in liberal society an
awareness of social justice, implemented by government
on behalf of all the people, limiting and regulating the
power of the wealthy.

Contrariwise, the liberal world drove home to
Marxist movements and regimes the ideological character of their own humanism, lacking as it did any pro-
vision for controlling the power of the party or the
government, or any freedom for dissent. It produced a
socialist movement that broke with communist abso-
lutism and became a force for change in democratic

society. In competition for human allegiance, challenged and leavened by Christian critique and participation, each ideology was held to a more realistic view of human nature and a more insightful, less scientific standard of human and social truth than either would have realized alone.

Now the competition is over. The communist world has collapsed, victim of its own misplaced ideals and its unrealism about human drives and motivations. Democratic socialist forces are unsure of their message, partly due to their past success in achieving social reforms, partly due to their own, too materialist humanism. Free enterprise capitalism is triumphant. Its rationality operates throughout the world despite local resistance from some non-Western cultures. But this rationality is self-contained and instrumental. Lacking effective challenge, it need no longer enter the stewardship of the environment, the welfare of the poor, or the values of traditional cultures into its calculations. Its ideological priests still try to justify it in terms of broader social vision, but these priests are functional only as they help rationalize policies based on profitability and risk management. A postmodern economy functions, until its markets collapse or catastrophe intervenes, without a truth claim other than its own success.

Meanwhile, the excluded protest, but ineffectually. No ideology unites them. They too have become postmodern. A subsistence culture here, a poor nation there, a city ghetto, an immigrant population, a racial minority, and recently groups united by sexual orientation—all try to assert themselves, but the truths they affirm are fragmented. They come across as self-assertions with no more validity than those of the dominant establishment.

Is there a word of God for this condition? There has been. It was clearer when the ideological conflict was more active and one could confront humanist faith with Christian faith in their implications for public policy. The social teachings of the World Council of Churches, the Roman Catholic Church, and many other denominations over the past century are rich resources for a realistic social vision that includes and transcends the truths which the ideological antagonists represent. Today the broad inclusive systems of theory and practice which we have called ideologies have been dismantled, but in the swept and empty room other devils, smaller but less responsible than they, have taken residence. There is still a world economy, and complex rationalizations of its operations. Against it, in it, and with it, hundreds of other groups, national, religious, cultural, and social, proclaim and fight for their survival with their own ideologies. The promise of God and the influence of the gospel are at work also here. To discern and make known how this is so, how human truths are affirmed, judged, relativized, in the midst of these struggles, is a form of Christian mission.

Third, it is commonly said by postmodern thinkers that Western culture has lost its metanarrative. It once had a truth framework, a structure of customs and common values, of meaningful beliefs—in a general sense, a common spiritual language. Now this is being attacked and dismantled. In many areas it has disappeared from common memory and experience. This is perhaps so, but what is the metanarrative that we are losing? Against the background of what history is this development so new and disturbing? Let us take a step back to gain perspective. David Bosch described the modern condition as the clash of two inconsistent plausibility structures: one influenced and molded by the Christian faith and the gospel story; the other by the mechanistic assumptions of scientific humanism. The historic metanarrative already had a cracked foundation. What held it together for so long was a sense of mature responsibility for a secularized world that did not have metaphysical or religious roots of its own. Dietrich Bonhoeffer, in one of the most influential books of the past half-century, put it thus:

> The movement that began about the thirteenth century (I'm not going to get involved in any argument about the exact date) towards the autonomy of humankind (in which I should include the discovery of the laws by which the world lives and deals with itself in science, social and political matters, art, ethics, and religion) has in our time reached an undoubted completion. Humans have learned to deal with themselves in all questions of importance without recourse to the "working hypothesis" called "God." In questions of science, art, and ethics this has become an understood thing at which one now hardly dares to tilt. But for the last hundred years or so it has also become increasingly true of religious questions…. As in the scientific field, so in human affairs generally, "God" is being pushed more and more out of life, losing more and more ground.

> …The world that has become conscious of itself and the laws that govern its own existence has grown self-confident in what seems to us an

uncanny way. False developments and failures do not make the world doubt the necessity of the course that it is taking, or of its development; they are accepted with fortitude and detachment as part of the bargain, and even an event like the present war [World War II] is no exception (1972:325–26, inclusive language added by the author).

This is secularization. It is the self-confident logic of the scientific method without its humanist faith. It repudiates religion, that is, "God" as a metaphysical security blanket to explain the world or as a means of salvation from it. But it does not do so on the basis of any philosophy, humanist or otherwise, of cosmic order or human salvation. It is, to quote a definition formulated by an ecumenical conference years ago, "the withdrawal of areas of life and thought from religious— and finally also from metaphysical—control and the attempt to understand and live in these areas in the terms which they alone offer" (West 1959:1).

It is important to note what is not being said here. Secularization is a process, not a worldview. It may be accompanied by various ideologies and philosophies that place it in a hopeful light, but its essence is a change in the method of human thought and action. Total coherence of reality is no longer its goal. Rather, various sciences live side by side, each useful in its field, each happy to establish cross-connections with others, but each seeking to solve the problems to which its method is appropriate. Secularization means loss of a coherent world, concentration on specialized areas and on what works. Bonhoeffer calls it a mature (*mündige*) world, or in the usual translation, a world come of age; a problem-solving world in which people take responsibility for themselves, each other, and society without depending on a philosophy or religion for security and rescue.

Bonhoeffer lived in such a world. His father and much of the German intelligentsia to which his father belonged embodied it. In the resistance to Hitler he saw conservative nationalists, liberal humanists, and Marxist socialists alike emerge from the destroyed shelters of their worldviews to risk their lives together in a responsible secular effort to save civilization from the Nazis. He felt and respected the integrity of this world; he wanted to confront it with Christ in its maturity and strength, not in its weakness and dependency. "I should like to speak of God," he wrote, "not on the boundaries but at the center, not in weaknesses but in strength; and therefore not in death and guilt but in [human] life and goodness.... God's 'beyond' is not the beyond of our cognitive faculties. The transcendence of epistemological theory has nothing to do with the transcendence of God. God is beyond in the midst of our life. The church stands, not at the boundaries where human powers give out, but in the middle of the village" (1972:282).

How does one speak of God in such a world? Not by attacking its problem-solving spirit, not by undermining the self-confidence of its maturity, but by calling it to true responsibility. "Here is the decisive difference between Christianity and all religions. Man's religiosity makes him look in his distress to the power of God in the world: God is the *deus ex machina*. The Bible directs human beings to God's powerlessness and suffering; only the suffering God can help. To that extent we may say that the development towards the world's coming of age outlined above, which has done away with a false conception of God, opens up a way of seeing the God of the Bible, who wins power and space in the world by his weakness. This will probably be the starting-point for our 'secular interpretation'" (1972:361, inclusive language added by the author).

Bonhoeffer knew that the gospel is no less a scandal to this mature, secularized—we might add postmodern—world than to any other. It is still a self-centered world that seeks to secure itself and expand its own well-being. Christ the crucified servant is hardly the solution to its problems that responsible managers and strategists are looking for. But the deck has been cleared of false refuges and securities. The relation of God's truth to human power, of God's covenant to human desires, can be posed clearly and without illusions. It is a world thrown back upon human relations as the reality of life, however they may be distorted by human sin. Pilate touched the edge of such a world with his ironic yet probing question. Countless twentieth-century people, trying to cope with their responsibilities in a world without metanarrative, have found Bonhoeffer's insight and his gospel helpful.

Still we must ask, has the world so come of age as Bonhoeffer perceived? Can human beings live in the concrete realities of human relations and find truth and meaning there, without reaching for some structure that will save them and promise them victory over the forces that threaten them within and without? Bonhoeffer seems to have assumed among the men and women in his mature world a personal integrity, a love of the world like his own, an awareness of its fragility, and a readiness to take responsibility for it, however distorted by self-centered bias that responsibility might be. But the acids of ideological suspicion have eaten deeply into the structure of this responsibility since his time. Philosophical deconstructionists have continued Marx's attack on the objectivity of truth but have extended it to the complete relativity of all structures of knowledge, all historical narratives, all ethics, and indeed all systems of meaning. Some see this as a liberation of human desires and passions from the repressive limitations of alien truth structures; others see it as the self producing itself by overcoming the constraints of socially conditioned knowledge. In any case, the result is complete diversity. The sociologist Zygmunt Bauman sums up the movement thus:

> The main feature ascribed to "postmodernity" is the permanent and irreducible pluralism of cultures, communal traditions, ideologies, "forms of life" or "language games"... or awareness and recognition of such pluralism. Things which are plural in the postmodern world cannot be arranged in an evolutionary sequence, or be seen as each other's inferior or superior stages; neither can they be classified as "right" or "wrong" solutions to common problems. No knowledge can be assessed outside the context of the culture, tradition, language game, etc., which makes it possible and endows it with meaning. Hence no criteria of validation are available which could be themselves justified "out of context." Without universal standards, the problem of the postmodern world is not how to globalize superior culture, but how to secure communication and mutual understanding between cultures (1992:102; quoted in Adams 1997:4–18).

So, not even an awareness of common human problems for which to take responsibility is still there. A "patchwork of minority discourses" is left, multiple forms of knowledge that fit no overall pattern. On what basis, then, can communication and understanding among them be developed? Jürgen Habermas suggests that "communicative action" is the key. What is no longer possible in concepts and theories as such may still happen in human praxis, and a theory of the dynamic of this praxis may be a new path to truth. But this still assumes a "modern" confidence in human reason finding its own transcultural criteria in itself. The problem with postmodern philosophy is, in Bosch's words, that "on the one hand the autonomy of reason is rejected; on the other, this is done solely by means of reason" (1995:24).

What is actually happening in the praxis of our culture goes in the opposite direction from Habermas's hopes, especially in the United States of America. Pragmatism—finding truth in the experience of success through experimental living—has always been both an American philosophy and an American habit of mind. It sounds deconstructionist, but there is nothing postmodern about it. The pragmatists' assumptions were basically humanist and liberal: that truth, justice, and cooperative patterns of human community would arise out of the practice of living together and producing the future. Even the power struggles of democratic society did not dim their confidence; it only helped them to tie conflict theory into their formula for progress. In the past few years, however, the loss of a controlling common objective—a sense of truth, justice, and humanity that all can share—has dissolved the framework of this confidence. The language of human rights, of equal opportunity, and of common citizenship in a land of promise, is still used; but the content of this language has been so reconstructed that various communities of discourse mean quite different realities by it. On the one side, a generation ago the forces of social change had one agenda, of which the war on poverty, racial integration, freedom of expression, and nondiscrimination on the basis of race, sex, religion, or any other difference were part. Today there are many movements, among women, African Americans, Hispanics, Asian Americans, the disabled, the working poor, and many more, each defining a particular group, its struggle, and its interests. These groups have had varying success in winning power, status, and security for their members. What they have lost is the metanarrative, the overarching sense of a truth that holds them all together and challenges the status quo in the name of true community. Postmodernism in practice not only destroys truth; it also promotes conformity to the status quo, however meaningless, for lack of a convincing alternative.

On the other side, the same thing is happening. Science, once the bastion of objectivity, is being pressed into the service of corporations and other agencies with the power to finance and therefore control the direction of research and the technology to make use of it. Think tanks have arisen that produce analyses and propose social policies in the name of truth, that serve the interests of those economic and political powers that have the wealth to fund them. On a more popular level, radio and television present various images of and perspectives on the common life as their advertisers and their search for a mass market

dictate, with no principle of selection except profit. The
result is impressions presented in simplified forms
designed to influence rather than convince public opinion, to reflect rather than to clarify public confusion.
Craig van Gelder suggests three consequences of all this:

   1. The multiplication of choices and the frag-
   mentation of meaning in an essentially meaningless world;

   2. The substitution of images in a rapidly changing context, without depth or lasting quality, for
   the actual realities of life;

   3. The radical immediacy of experienced reality
   in a constant process of change, to which both
   history and the broader dimensions of society
   seem irrelevant (Hunsberger and van Gelder
   1996:33).

   To these, should be added a fourth consequence—
the increasing capacity of organized economic powers
to influence and confuse public perceptions of reality
in service of their own ends.
   This is the fate of truth in our postmodern world.
The public responds to it all with suspicion and cynicism, but at the same time with judgments that, for
lack of a trusted point of reference, are often confused
and prejudiced. Our culture is losing its epistemological roots. If we cannot trust our informers, where do
we go to find truth? If there is no metanarrative, no
context of meaning, what can control and direct our
reactions, our desires, or our fears?

## Pilate's Question, Revisited

What, then, is truth for this postmodern world? One can discern a pattern here. As modern truth was a humanist distortion of the gospel and at the same time a justified reaction against the illegitimate union that the church blessed of biblical revelation with a form of Greek cosmology, so postmodern truth is a relativist distortion of humanity and at the same time a justified reaction against the claims of scientific humanism, maintained by the powers of industry and technology, to know and control all reality. The Holy Spirit is also at work here, amid all the cynicism, the will to power, the doubts and the fears that compose its ethos. To suggest how, we return to the fourfold description of truth in the biblical heritage.

First, postmodernism has, by the grace of God, closed every door to Christian apologetics. The ways by which Christianity earlier accommodated itself to the Enlightenment worldview, in the effort to be more persuasive to it on its terms, are not open to us. Postmodernism claims to have no worldview, no structure of coherent truth. We must take it at its word and behavior. There is here no covert unifying faith. In its pluralistic relativism, it bears witness to a basic Christian insight: no human system of thought or behavior can capture and codify the word of God. There is no way by which the human mind, with its own resources, can formulate absolute truth. Karl Barth, the first postmodern theologian, put it clearly: "There is no way from us to God, not even a *via negativa,* not even a *via dialectica or paradoxa.* The god who stood at the end of some human way—even these ways—would not be God" (1957:177). Truth, the whole truth that claims the human mind, emotion, and will, begins with the revelation of God and the calling of human beings into faith and obedience. It confronts the postmodern world not with another structure of truth, but with One who gives and commands here and now.

Postmodernity has cleared the decks of false universals so that this claim may at least be heard. The decks are still cluttered, of course, with unconnected realms of discourse, with countless fleeting images, multiple areas of choice, and a sense of the relativity—and therefore meaninglessness—of them all. There is profound and understandable suspicion of any attempt to impose order on all this chaos. God's word does not attempt to do so. Rather, it calls us out of ourselves—our subjective experiences and choices, our divided and therefore finally meaningless "language games"—into true, that is, faithful and responsible, action in the midst of it all, toward the humanity revealed in Christ. It legitimates the secular, problem-solving ethos of the "world come of age" as a secular, and therefore fallible, effort of sinful humanity to create a relatively just, humane, and peaceful community. It confronts all such efforts with the judging and redeeming work of Christ. It invites us to live by faith in God's truth, which relativizes and gives direction to the fragments of meaning with which we live.

Second, the Christian message invites the world to look for truth in quite a different place from that which postmodernist philosophy and culture have repudiated. The deconstructionists may be relatively right or relatively wrong in finding that there are no longer any universal categories, any general standards, that bring together the separate fields of discourse and behavior in a pluralist society. The point is that truth is not to be found in the search for those universals, but in the relationship which God has established with human beings through the work of the Holy Spirit in Jesus Christ. Not the generally recognized rational structure which all acknowledge is true, but the One who has created us, called us, made covenant with us, forgiven us when we have gone astray, made us new in the church, and promised us a new creation in the victory of Christ over the powers of this world. The objective reality we seek with our reason (modernity) and finally give up on (postmodernity) is replaced by the living Other whom we can never control but to whom we respond by trust and discipleship. Truth is the character, the action, and, in an inclusive sense, the word of this God.

We are invited to explore the world, of nature and of human affairs, in and through this relationship. Habermas, Bauman and others are right in naming communication among fragmented thought and life structures as the basic problem of postmodern society. Our calling is to discern how Christ takes form in all of them and in their relations with one another. In so doing we will discover flexible, open, and changing forms of community and will work to keep them open to the challenge of outsiders and of God.

This is a process of discovery, repentance, and transformation that will end only on the final judgment day. We are not the managers of God's truth. We will never know it all without distortion until that day comes. But meanwhile we are in this truth. We are witnesses to it. We are communicators to a skeptical world of a divine truth in human form, whose mystery we can explore but never control even with our logic or our doctrine.

Third, Christians know, more profoundly than the most radical cynic, about the ideological distortion in all human truth claims. It infects even the way the church proclaims and interprets the truth of the gospel, as we have seen at every stage of history from New Testament times until now. Karl Marx was prophetic in his analysis of much Christian religion— that it both sanctifies the dominant culture and provides an illusory escape from its oppressions and inhumanities. If the word of God is not heard in the postmodern world, one reason is that too many believers distort the truth by a false relation. On the one hand, truth claims may become a closed circle of morals and language that does not take part in Christ's transforming work in the cultures and worlds beyond their immediate personal communities. On the other hand, they may imitate the patterns of the postmodern mood with their own depthless images and momentary experiences, vying for attention in the media market. In either case they become one more among the competing centers in an essentially meaningless world.

The truth of God, the gospel of Jesus Christ, begins with the justification of sinful humanity in all its self-centered expressions, including religion, ideology, and postmodern pluralism. All human truths are under judgment, the judgment of a redeeming God who forgives by placing us in a new relationship, with a new perspective. In this new relationship we live by grace, not by our own virtue. We are therefore empowered to risk being witnesses to God's truth in the daily business of life, to name false spirits and unjust powers when we discern them, to invite others to follow Christ, knowing that in so doing we are open to correction and change by God's word and by our fellow human beings, whether believers or not. The truth of God is trustworthy; it judges all our lies and redeems us all, Christians and nonbelievers.

Fourth, the God who made a covenant with the Jews in the wilderness of Sinai and who came on earth in Jesus Christ is at work in postmodern society no less than in previous more ideological or religious ages. Truth is concrete and historical, now as then. Our task is one of discernment. To put it plainly, the truths of science and technology, the truths of economic power and development, the truths of responsible justice and ordering in a world without religion, the truths of advocacy groups and the fragmented shards of truth to which deconstructed postmodernists cling are all meaningful and promising in the context of God's faithfulness and God's promise. This is the historical direction that legitimates and controls them all. Human destiny has the form of Christ the servant, the crucified, and the risen Lord. This is the truth of history. Secular truths, of science, of economics, of government, of social justice, and of human selfhood, are valid as they serve and express it.

# 2

# The Gospel as Community

Now there were dwelling in Jerusalem Jews, devout men from every nation under heaven. And at this sound the multitude came together, and they were bewildered, because each one heard [the apostles] speaking in his own language. And they were amazed and wondered, saying, "Are not all these who are speaking Galileans? And how is it that we hear, each of us in his own native language? Parthians and Medes and Elamites and residents of Mesopotamia, Judea and Cappadocia, Pontus and Asia, Phrygia and Pamphylia, Egypt and the parts of Libya belonging to Cyrene, and visitors from Rome, both Jews and proselytes, Cretans and Arabians, we hear them telling in our own tongues the mighty works of God." And all were amazed and perplexed, saying to one another, "What does this mean?" (Acts 2:5–12)

What does it mean—then and now? One thing is clear: in that event, where the Holy Spirit made every human language open to the transforming word of God, the church was born. It received its ecumenical mission. Not all who heard responded; but those who did, both Jews and Gentiles, became a community of service and witness to the nations, ambassadors of Christ in God's reconciliation of the world. They were both one church, called out of their many nations into the household of God and free citizens who could express God's saving promise in and for the language, customs, and culture of their own peoples, in their human households. How can we live the gospel this way? If we succeed, what kind of a society will we produce?

### The Promise and the Problem

The question is not new. It flows from sources deep in the biblical history before the calling of Abraham. The generations of the sons of Noah, the Bible says, spread abroad on the earth after the flood "in their lands, each with his own language (tongue [Hebrew: *tongoe*]), by their families, in their nations" (Gen. 10:5; cf. vv. 20, 31). This was good. After hunting and farming, it was the first human response to God's covenant with Noah. It elaborated the basic human relationships between the first couple in the Garden of Eden, which God had created and blessed. Families, peoples, languages, and lands are the diverse forms in which people organize their lives and develop their cultures. They are historical. They are human responses, not revealed orders of creation. They arise, have their day, and play their role. They shift, change, and eventually disappear, to be replaced by other forms. As such they are blessed and bear witness in their time and place to the covenant promise of God.

The very next chapter of the book of Genesis, however, tells a different story.

> The whole earth had one language (Hebrew "lip," not "tongue") and few words. And as [people] migrated from the east, they found a plain in the land of Shinar and settled there. And they said to one another, "Come, let us make bricks, and burn them thoroughly." And they had brick for stone, and bitumen for mortar. Then they said, "Come, let us build ourselves a city, and a tower with its top in the heavens, and let us make a name for ourselves, lest we be scattered abroad upon the face of the whole earth" (Gen. 11:1–4).

Many motives seem to have driven the citizens of what came to be known as Babel. Most of them are still at work in society today: pride—the desire to reach the heavens by their own efforts; lust for economic and political power—the desire to make a name for themselves that would impress and intimidate all others; or fear—the search for security against being divided and scattered. In any case, they sacrificed real community for a human construction. Diversity of language, culture, and nation became for them a thing to be resisted. The spreading that God had blessed was feared as "scattering." The community of a city and a tower became protection against the blessed but less secure community of different peoples with one another and with God. The fear was self-fulfilling. Tongues that had understood one another when they talked about human relations and response to God became confused languages when human ambition and human fear drove their discourse. So the peoples were scattered, not just spread "abroad over the face of all the earth" (11:9) into nations, each of whose cultures was incomprehensible and therefore enemy to all the others.

This biblical story—legendary perhaps, but true—describes the underlying problem of human community then and ever since. The German scholar Gerhard van Rad writes:

> It shows how human beings, in their striving for fame, solidarity, and expansion of their own power, have set themselves against God and suffer the punishment for it. They, who are so concerned for unity and togetherness, lie now scattered in a confusion where they can no longer understand one another…. So, universal history seems to break up in shrill dissonance, and the urgent question is posed: is God's relation to the peoples finally broken? Is God's gracious patience finally exhausted? Has God rejected the nations in anger forever? This is the burdensome question that no thoughtful reader of Genesis Chapter 11 can avoid. Indeed one can say that our storyteller intends to demonstrate this question in all its severity, in the whole plot of this early history. Only then is the reader rightly prepared to take in the strange newness of what follows the bleak Babel story: the election, and the promised blessing of Abraham (1956:149).

There is no easy transition here; there never is between analysis of the human condition, with consequences that everyone can recognize, and the incomprehensible promise of God. Abram, one of the descendants of Shem with no special virtue, was simply chosen and sent: "Go from your country and your kindred and your father's house to the land that I will show you. I will make of you a great nation, and I will bless you, and make your name great, so that you will be a blessing.... [A]nd in you all the families of the earth shall be blessed" (Gen. 12:1–3 NRSV). The parallel is striking. What the people of Babel feared most is laid on the grandfather of Israel as a calling: "Go from your country and your kindred." What for the Babelites was a curse is for Abram the promise of a blessing. He would be father of a great nation; his name would be great. But the greatness of this nation would be not its culture and power, but its faithfulness to the covenant and its witness only to the merciful power of God. Through the response and covenant obedience of this one wandering people, all the families of the earth would be blessed.

How does one nation fulfill a calling like this? How can a people, with a culture, a language, a tradition, and a territory, be at the same time an instrument of God's reconciliation of all peoples in a community that embraces every culture and nation? The Jewish people, from the time of Moses to the present, have wrestled with this question. It lies at the heart of their existence as a chosen and covenant people. They have bequeathed their struggle, and their witness, to the Christian church, which responds to the same God.

The way is beset by temptations. On the one side lies the imperialist answer. One culture, usually expressed in one religion and one language, supported by one political authority, supplies the unifying force— usually, though not always, by conquest. Other peoples, languages, and religions may exist under its suzerainty, but only the dominant culture sets the standards, maintains the order, and keeps the peace. Such was the pattern of ancient Egypt, of Babylon, of the Chinese Empire and civilization, of Greek culture in the Hellenic Empires, and of the civilization established and ruled by Rome. Israel was at least tempted to move in this direction in the days of David and Solomon. Medieval civilization in Europe, Orthodox in the east and Roman Catholic in the west, gave full-blown, if always troubled, expression to it. So did Islam, which confronted it with another imperium. Elements of it are ambiguously present in our age, in nineteenth-century Western imperialism, and are disguised in the technological and economic ethos of late twentieth-century globalization.

On the other side lies religious nationalism—one culture that becomes itself a sacred sphere where God is known and worshiped and for which other nations are by their existence at best strangers, at worst threats or enemies. Such was the pattern in the ancient Near East. The children of Abraham fell into it far too often despite the prophets' protests, as Old Testament history testifies. Nor has the Christian church been free of the temptation, as the religious wars in Europe over the centuries, the current conflicts in Northern Ireland and in former Yugoslavia, and Christian nationalism in Russia, the United States, and elsewhere today bear eloquent witness. It should not be surprising that there are also modern pagan (Nazi, Fascist) and self-righteous American expressions of it.

The people of Israel were given a different mission—to find their way between these fatal rocks on one or the other of which so many cultures have foundered, toward a new vision of human community inspired by the promise of God. For this they were, to begin with, a chosen people. They brought no power of their own to this choice. "It was not because you were more in number than any other people that the LORD set his love upon you and chose you, for you were the fewest of all peoples; but it is because the LORD loves you" (Deut. 7:7–8a). They owed their existence and their rescue from Egypt to God's calling, mercy, and faithfulness, and to nothing else. They owed the form and meaning of their life to God's justice and to the covenant and the law that expressed it. "Now therefore, if you will obey my voice and keep my covenant, you shall be my own possession among all peoples; for all the earth is mine, and you shall be to me a kingdom of priests and a holy nation" (Exod. 19:5–6a).

In this context they were heirs to a boundless promise: posterity, land, victory over enemies, economic prosperity, and, not least, inspiration and leadership among all the other nations. "Keep [the statutes and ordinances of the Lord] and do them; for that will be your wisdom and your understanding in the sight of the peoples, who, when they hear all these statutes, will say, 'Surely this great nation is a wise and understanding people,'" (Deut. 4:6).

They were also a nation under judgment for not keeping faith with this covenant. In fact, this unfaithfulness and God's judgment on it were even stronger witness than their ideals to the way in which God shapes what a nation should be. The people turned to other gods—gods of their neighbors or gods of their own making—for security and success. They depended

on military power and political alliances and not on
God for protection. In their prosperity they were deaf
to the cry of the poor for justice. In all of this, as the
prophets drove home to them, they brought destruction on themselves. "You only have I known of all the
families of the earth," thunders the prophet Amos,
"therefore I will punish you for all your iniquities"
(3:2). This is the other side of being chosen to be the
bearer of the promise of God.

It is also not the end of the story. Conquered and
exiled, Israel is invited to be, in its weakness, an
instrument of the power of God:

> "Behold my servant, whom I uphold,
>     my chosen, in whom my soul delights;
> I have put my Spirit upon him,
>     he will bring forth justice to the nations.
> He will not cry or lift up his voice,
>     or make it heard in the street;
> a bruised reed he will not break,
>     and a dimly burning wick he will not quench;
>     he will faithfully bring forth justice.
> He will not fail or be discouraged
>     till he has established justice in the earth;
>     and the coastlands wait for his law." (Isa. 42:1–4)

Justice, the fabric of community, is established by the
servant, not the master. Through this servant, God
reaches out from one people to include all peoples in
the community of justice, mercy, and truth, which is
God's covenant (Isa. 49:6–12). To be a culture, a community, a nation for other nations is the calling of the
people of Abraham and Moses.

So it has been through the centuries until now. The Jewish people in diaspora, spread among the nations of the world, have by their very existence borne witness that those nations, their power and their culture, are not ultimate. Another people, chosen by God and formed by God's covenant, lives among them, challenges them with its culture and its law even without political power of its own, an implicit reminder of God's commandment, judgment, and mercy on us all. The nations, even those that claim to be Christian, have not taken kindly to this reminder. Cultures do not like to be confronted with their relativity and their need to learn from strangers who are in their midst. The Holocaust is only the most extreme reaction they have produced. Forced segregation in the ghetto is centuries old. So is discrimination, undergirded by suspicion and fear. Still the challenge continues. The Jews are a nation, not just in Israel but everywhere. Like others, they struggle to maintain their culture, their language, and in Israel, their land. But they are also a covenant people, and therefore are not like other nations. They are a witness to every nation of its place in the community of all peoples who are called into covenant with one another and with God.

## The Consequences of Pentecost

It is no accident that the listeners at Pentecost were Jews and proselytes—Gentiles drawn to the God whom the Jews worshiped—from the diaspora. They knew the history of their people. They shared the covenant and its promise. They looked for the salvation of Israel. At the same time, they belonged also to the cultures of the lands where they lived. They spoke the languages of those lands. They knew from sad experience that those languages, like all those after Babel, were not channels but barriers to outsiders and other cultures. They were sources of division, not peace. These people were in Jerusalem to seek something more universal, a community embracing the *oikoumene*, the whole inhabited world. The Greek spoken in the marketplace was ecumenical in this sense, but it was too shallow a community. The Latin of their governors was a political *oikoumene* (Luke 2:1), noble in the universality of its law, but it expressed the culture of their conquerors. In their own flesh they experienced the dilemma of their people—one nation called to be faithful to the covenant in all the aspects of life and at the same time to witness to a God who wills to establish his covenant with all nations and all cultures.

Into this rootless and diverse community, united only in tradition and faith, came the Pentecost event. Simple Galileans, people from a limited nation like their own, spoke to each of them clearly in his or her native language about the mighty works of God. Each dialect had become once more a tongue, as before the time of Babel. Then they were ready to hear the preaching of Peter that in one man—a Jew, Jesus of Nazareth, crucified and risen from the dead—God had fulfilled his promise to the people of Israel and was drawing them with other peoples into a new community of hope.

Two results follow from all of this. First, the household of God, of which Christ is the head, grows out of the Jewish nation. Its mission to all peoples is a new direction in the history of God with the covenant people that began with the calling of Abraham. We cannot therefore separate the gospel in the New Testament from this particular history. The same Triune God, maker of the heavens and the earth, whom we know in Christ and the Holy Spirit, is the one who calls, promises, guides, judges, and redeems the covenant people through the Old Testament as well. Through God's relationship with this one nation, words like justice, mercy, peace, and love become concrete. The gospel of Jesus Christ for all nations, the gospel of repentance, forgiveness, salvation, and hope, is given form and human substance.

Second, in Christ the desire of all nations (Hag. 2:7), including the Jews, has indeed been fulfilled and at the same time transformed. It was an old man named Simeon, led by the Spirit to come to the temple when a poor Galilean couple were bringing their child Jesus "to do for him according to the custom of the law" (Luke 2:27), who said it first:

> "Lord, now lettest thou thy servant depart in peace,
>> according to thy word;
>> for mine eyes have seen thy salvation
>> which thou hast prepared in the presence
>> of all peoples, a light for revelation to the
>> nations [Greek: *ethné*],
>> and for glory to thy people Israel."
> (Luke 2:29–32)

Israel has been relieved of the intolerable burden of trying to be, with its own law, its own culture, its own language, and its own religious-political structure, the only community that expresses God's covenant and promise. Its history and its hope are taken up into the new reality of God incarnate in one of Israel's prophet-teachers, who was executed and rose from the dead to head a new community of people from all the nations, who brought to all nations in their languages and cultures the good news of their salvation. This is the glory of Israel. Religious nationalism, with all its pride and illusions, has been purged. In its place we have the Triune God at work through the community of Christ's church—the new *oikoumene*, blessing every culture in its time and place, calling each to repentance, faith, discipleship, and to a hope no culture can give to itself. This is the light of revelation to the nations. For the relation of universal, ecumenical community to the many communities of the world, it means:

a. *The gospel penetrates every human culture with the covenant promise of God*. It is, to use Lamin Sanneh's words, inherently translatable (Sanneh 1990). The Hebrew of the Old Testament and the koiné Greek of the Roman Empire marketplace in which the New Testament was written are God's instruments, but they are not sacred. The word of God finds expression, faithful to the biblical history and message, in the life and idiom of each nation to which it comes. It brings that culture into the history of God's work, which began with the children of Abraham and was fulfilled in the life, death, and resurrection of Jesus Christ, as the biblical story tells. But that work continues and will continue through the diverse cultures and languages of many societies until the final consummation of all things. Christ, whom we know from the New Testament story, takes form in and for every people, in every language. The plurality of their witnesses, the creative diversity of their cultures, is part of the church's testimony to the depth and fullness of the covenant purpose of God.

b. *The gospel transforms and renews the cultures into which it comes.* The biblical story of God's dealing with the Hebrew people is the original paradigm for this. But every encounter is a drama of its own. It may involve bringing a great philosophical or religious tradition into the historical drama, as happened in the early centuries of the church when it wrestled with the Greek philosophical world, or is happening now as the church faces Hinduism in India or Buddhist and Confucian traditions in Korea, China, or Japan. It may happen, as Sanneh has documented, in Africa, when the Bible is translated into a rich but unwritten language, creating a renewal of that culture as it interacts with the word of God. It may follow when a pagan ruler, to enhance his power or enrich his domain, decides to adopt Christianity, with consequences that change forever the culture of the people he leads and his own place as leader. The first millennium of Christian history is filled with such examples. In any case, what can result is a renewed nation, confident in its own creativity, at home in its language and ways of life, yet always aware of the ecumenical community that the church embodies and therefore open to change in encounter with other cultures and with God.

c. *The gospel secularizes cultures and the nations that embody them.* Religious nationalism is idolatry. No culture, no human way of life, is sacred. This is the lesson that Israel learned at the cost of wandering, warfare, exile, and conquest over centuries. It is the lesson that Christian peoples have to learn over and over again. God alone is ultimate; human responses to God are penultimate. They are relative, limited human efforts to realize in history some degree of justice, freedom, prosperity, and peace. But this is salvation for the nations in all their diversity. No longer must they make a name for themselves lest they be scattered abroad across the face of the earth. A community of communities is once more possible on earth, because no human community is eternal or absolute. Nations, cultures, even languages can change in interaction with one another. Problems can be solved by negotiation and compromise. Diversity is blessed in its relative secularity by the presence of Christ in and for this world.

d. *The gospel saves cultures from self-destruction by bringing them into the sphere of God's justification and sanctification.* It confronts every nation with a new reality, the crucified and risen Christ in its midst. It is a reality of both judgment and hope; of judgment on all the self-centered pride, fear, and oppression by which a culture closes in on itself and excludes not only the outsider but also the poor in its midst; of hope because repentance and forgiveness are possible also for nations who seek justice and peace, even at risk of security, in their own societies and with other peoples. "In Christ God was reconciling the world to himself, not counting their trespasses against them" (2 Cor. 5:19). This way lies the future for every nation.

e. *The church—the community of believers, the household of God, and the body of Christ—is the messenger of all this and is its first embodiment.* It carries within itself the interaction between the one ecumenical community of all peoples and the plurality of communities in which the world also lives. Its mission is to discern and bear witness to how Christ takes form in each culture—in the tensions and conflicts between cultures and in the events of history that change and threaten them. Its worship points all cultures toward the one community that embraces, redeems, and gives hope to them all.

## Community, Christendom, and Mission

For two thousand years both the church and the world have been wrestling with this gospel and with their relation to each other in the light of its promise. Jesus was born into an imperial society. It was assumed that the world of culture and civilization, the *oikoumene*, was the Roman Empire, though there were peoples on its borders and outside it. In this world there was one language of government and law, Latin; another of commerce, Greek; and a shared culture with differences of emphasis that could be expressed in either language. For the church, this was both opportunity and temptation. The universality of the claim of Christ could be more easily understood in a world where particular nations were subordinate politically to Rome, linguistically to Greek and Latin, and culturally to the major forms of Hellenistic philosophy, literature, and religion. The task of making disciples of the people of one great civilization, though mammoth, was at least in its broad outlines clear.

But the reality, especially as Rome decayed, was more complex. Already in the first two centuries the Christian mission spread beyond the limits of the Graeco-Roman *oikoumene* to Edessa, in Parthian lands, which became the first Christian city-state in the third century, to Armenia, which became a

Christian nation in 304 A.D., to India, Ethiopia, and other points south and east. Furthermore, it was evident to missionaries that peoples within the empire, from the Copts in Egypt to the Celts in Britain, needed to hear and respond to the gospel in their own languages, reviving and transforming their own cultures in the encounter. To this must be added that the imperium itself divided into a Roman west and a Byzantine east. The church held together longer than the empire did, but then it too divided, on theological grounds, but also for cultural, linguistic, and political reasons.

Out of this emerged the peculiar combination of gospel with human culture known as Christendom, which has dominated the history of the Western world from the fall of Rome until modern times. Indeed, in many parts of the world, and in many places in the hearts, minds, and cultural habits of Christians, it is still with us.

What is Christendom? Oliver O'Donovan, one of its staunchest defenders, defines it as "a historical idea: that is to say, the idea of a professedly Christian secular political order, and the history of that idea in practice. Christendom is an *era*, an era in which the truth of Christianity was taken to be a truth of secular politics" (1996:195). Dietrich Bonhoeffer, looking back from the cauldron of World War II, was more total: "Our own Christian past... is a historical heritage, a common western heritage. Jesus Christ has made of the west a historical unit.... The unity of the west is not an idea but a historical reality whose only foundation is Christ" (1992:98, my trans.).

Taking this broader view of it, there was for centuries a *corpus christianum* in which the whole of culture was formed by its relation in faith to the Triune God in its midst and the promise of the reign of Jesus Christ for its destiny. Culture, from the scholarly work of the monks to the rhythm of life in town and country, was formed in response to this God. Political power (the subject of the next chapter) was legitimized and corrected by its role under this authority. Trade and commerce, as they developed, found their function and their limits in this context.

About this era, especially in western Europe, an ocean of literature has been written, from many perspectives. But what does it mean for us today in our quest for gospel in community? Four thoughts suggest themselves.

1. The achievement of the church in Christianizing the cultures of Europe from the Caucasus to Spain and Ireland is a direct response to the command of Christ to "make disciples of all nations, baptizing them in the name of the Father and of the Son and of the Holy Spirit, teaching them to observe all that I have commanded you" (Matt. 28:19) and to Paul's commission to "preach to the nations the unsearchable riches of Christ" (Eph. 3:8). The risen Christ is Lord over the whole life of humankind, not just the few saved. The gospel is for the world, not just for the church. How Christ takes form there, how the world in all its communities can unite in praising God and living by the Spirit in all the dimensions of society, is the quest and the calling of mission. In fact, the mission of the early church did penetrate, permeate, and transform the cultures into which it came: first the dominant Hellenistic culture in both its Greek and Roman forms, then the

cultures of invading tribes. After the fall of Rome, it
became the culture-forming influence throughout
Europe, the basis for the coherence of medieval times.
Built into this was recognition that the church was captive to no one culture or nation, but that its liturgy, its
authority, and even the Latin language it used as the
vehicle of both culture and worship were expressions of
the unity of humankind in Christ under which various
cultures and languages could develop and flourish.
Plurality was built into this unity. A secular realm had
its relative autonomy. Its relation to the ecclesiastical
was always subject to negotiation, even involving,
sometimes, conflict.

2. However, the other side of this success was that
the relation between the community of faith and the
world changed fundamentally. In modern secular society, we are still trying to cope with the consequences
of that change. John Howard Yoder puts it thus:
"Before Constantine one knew as a fact of everyday
experience that there was a believing Christian community, but one had to 'take it on faith' that God was
governing history. After Constantine one had to
believe without seeing that there was a community of
believers within the larger nominally Christian mass,
but one knew for a fact that God was in control of history" (1984:137). The result, says Yoder, was twofold:
outwardly, to be Christian was to be part of this society and support the authorities, both civil and ecclesiastical; inwardly, it could mean to cultivate a special
religious life that went beyond, but did not challenge,
the Christianized structure of public order. But the
gospel itself could not be so contained. Christendom

has had to cope, from the beginning, with protests from within against the cultural, political, and sometimes even the liturgical and hierarchical expression of the reality and promise of God in the world. These have been both promising and disrupting. Sometimes, as with most of the monastic and friar orders, they have been contained by the church and have changed it from within. In other cases, as with the Albigensians and many other dualistic or apocalyptic groups, they have been suppressed, sometimes brutally. In still others, like the sixteenth-century Reformers, they have divided the Catholic Church in trying to reform it. Christendom, in other words, was constantly subject to protests and challenges that reminded it of the inadequacy and the corruption of its synthesis of church and society. Through these challenges it changed and grew. By these challenges it was also divided and wounded. We may not forget that the Thirty Years' War of the seventeenth century, which caused the death of 30 percent of the population of Germany, was fought to preserve a certain form of the unity of Christendom, and failed.

3. Christendom was divided almost from the beginning into an eastern (Greek) and a western (Latin) realm. Both the Byzantine church under the Ecumenical Patriarch and the Roman church under the Pope claimed ecumenicity and catholicity. Both realized it in their areas to some degree. But a line of conflict was drawn across Europe that has raged through the centuries, as Roman Catholic Poland and Lithuania fought Orthodox Russia and Ukraine. It still flares up today, in former Yugoslavia, for example, and in hostility over the claims of Greek Catholic, or uniate, churches with

Byzantine liturgy and Roman obedience. The very claim to universality has ironically intensified and made more brutal the battle of nations with each other.

4. Christendom, in building a certain form of unity in balance with the plurality of peoples and cultures in its realm, created a problem for the church in mission to other peoples, and to new forms of culture outside its sphere. The translatability of the gospel (Sanneh 1990) was undermined by the cultural terms in which it was expressed. Again, Yoder notes: "Once 'Christendom' means Empire, non-empire is a new challenge. The era of Charlemagne demonstrates the option of annexation and fusion. Germanic values, legal traditions, social structures, and ruling families are 'baptized' globally. This does not mean, at least for most of them, conversion in any deep sense. It means rather that the name of Jesus is now intoned over a Germanic culture without changing its inner content" (1984:137). This is too severe a judgment, but it makes a basic point. Christendom made Christian mission an instrument of imperial conquest over other cultures rather than of judgment and renewal. Christian churches, both Eastern Orthodox and Roman Catholic, became too much like Islam in confronting Islam with another union of culture, power, and faith, rather than with the promise and claim of Christ. There were missions, of course, by Orthodox churches to the peoples of central Asia, and by Catholics following the explorations and conquests of Spanish and Portuguese adventurers. But where they succeeded, it was more often a religious form of conquest than a penetration and renewal of culture in Christ. The churches of the Reformation

were, to their credit, highly critical of this, with the result, however, that for them Christendom turned inward and focused on the nation. Mission, as a dimension of Christian life, nearly disappeared from their agenda.

## The Gospel, Christianity, and the Individual

Today we are in a different world. Christendom is still a social structure on a few Pacific islands, the fruit of nineteenth-century missions. It persists as a state of mind in many traditionally Christian societies, including parts of the United States. It has even been revived as a nationalist dream in parts of eastern Europe. But only in the claims and structure of the Roman Catholic Church and the ethereal presence of pan-Orthodoxy does it reach over national boundaries. Nowhere is it unchallenged. It continues rather as one strand in a world of many communities and cultures and as one view among others of how the gospel, and therefore the church, relates to them.

Theologically, we can trace this breakdown—or emancipation—to the Reformation, even though the established churches of the Reformation were sometimes slow to learn it. It was Martin Luther who destroyed the medieval Catholic worldview of hierarchical continuity between human works and divine grace, laity and clergy, secular culture and ecclesiastical institutions. The world as he saw it is a battleground between God and the Devil, between the reign of Christ and sinful human desire for wealth, power, and self-righteousness. The Christian is righteous by God's justification alone, free in Christ to act creatively even as a sinner, knowing that God will both judge and redeem. Gospel and culture are therefore paradoxically related. Christians live in two realms. They are called to bear witness in the world to the way in which God in Christ both judges and transforms it. The church is the community of believers who, with only Christ as head, live this gospel.

Calvin and the Puritans who followed him carried this a step further. The Christian life for Calvin was a combination of self-denial in communion with Christ, with proper appreciation and use of the gifts of God in this world. Therefore the organization of human life and society for justice, peace, and relationships of mutual care, including the control and limitation of the effects of human sin, were the elements of Christian vocation, even though they involve the believer in relative, ambivalent actions that will need to be forgiven. Christians can take responsibility and bear witness in the secular sphere, but the church does not control it. Gospel and culture are therefore in a positive tension. The covenant of God with believers in the church should be the model for society: called to live as a company of sinners always being reformed by the word of God. The representative governance of the church from below can be a model for secular government. The form of mutual responsibility, forgiveness, and support among Christian believers can be a resource for guiding behavior in the world of commerce, business, neighborhood, and nation. In all of this the church works with the world as both responsible partner and as witness to the judging and transforming word of God over and for the world. Cultures and communities live, by the work of the church in their midst, in this confidence and this openness to judgment and change.

For some children of the Radical Reformation, to be sure, this relative and world-oriented understanding of the church has seemed much too mild a break with Christendom. The church itself must become a culture, the culture of the community committed to following Christ in all the dimensions of common life. The company of believers lives by faith in a quite different reality from the world—the reality of Christ's command and example, and of the divine kingdom that is coming and has already established itself among us. In the words of a modern advocate: "We must first of all confess," says Yoder, "—if we believe it—that the meaning of history lies not in the acquisition and defense of the culture and the freedoms of the West, not in the aggrandizement of material comforts and political sovereignty, but in the calling together 'for God saints from every tribe and language and people and nation,' a 'people of his own who are zealous for good deeds'" (1994:61). In this community, God redeems sinners by bringing them into this discipleship and calling. They participate in the nonviolent sacrifice and victory of Christ, and order life together in this obedience and hope. The world is outside this community. It "is neither all nature nor all humanity nor all 'culture'; it is *structured unbelief*, rebellion taking with it a fragment of what should have been the Order of the Kingdom" (62). This world is therefore not the object of responsible participation by Christians, though to serve humanity and prevent evil, they may sometimes serve in its structures, so far as their witness is not compromised. This world is under judgment. It will disappear when Christ comes to reign. The company of disciples, not the world, is where the coming reality is to be believed and lived.

Both forms of the Reformation share with centuries of preceding Christendom the belief that one church confronts one world with the judging and saving word of God. Unity is the first concern of them all. The proliferation of the world into various nations, languages, and cultures, and the problem of the church's witness to the gospel in and for many human communities is, for them, secondary. What has changed for the Reformers is the relation between church and world, and the operation of human sin and divine grace in both. The Radicals tear Christendom apart. The magisterial reformers secularize it. For the Radicals, unbelief embraces all the varieties of the world. Faith and discipleship unite the church in one form of life, one "culture," against them all. For Luther, Calvin, and the churches that followed them, the church becomes that part of the world where the gospel—the good news of God's judging and saving grace—for the world is heard and responded to. The world, with its nations and cultures, becomes the sphere of God's work bringing forth fruits in this age, among human sinners, as signs of the promise of the coming fulfillment of all things in Christ.

In any case, partly prepared by Reformation ecclesiology and church life, the world has gone its own way in the West toward pluralization. Old patterns of nation, language and culture have reemerged in new secular forms. Meanwhile, new divisions based on class status in the economic revolution have overshadowed them. From the late Middle Ages well into the seventeenth century, trade and commerce were assumed to be forms of the service of God to be governed by the moral discipline of the church for the welfare of the community. Greed, the lust for profit beyond reasonable return for a service, and exploitation of the needy in employment, trade, or finance were recognized as sin. Laws of just price and wage, of limits on loans at interest, of proper value in exchange were still enforceable in Calvin's Geneva, and even a century later in John Winthrop's Boston. In the years that followed, however, forces driving the commercial and later the industrial revolution broke out of the moral and spiritual control that the churches, both Roman Catholic and Protestant, had previously exercised over them. In Europe, the ancient parish system was disrupted. Peasants were driven from their land into industrial cities to form a new working class that the church never really penetrated. Christian spirituality became an individual matter. The communal responsibility of the church for the world weakened into moral exhortation to guide the private conscience. Meanwhile, a growing commercial and industrial economy followed its own ways, which had no relation to those of God, and offered a promise that had little to do with the gospel.

The social philosophy that drove this development was individualist humanism. It owed much to the Christendom it replaced—a lively hope for the human future, belief in the unique value of human beings and in a benevolent natural law undergirding the whole human enterprise. But its premise was, and still is, that the individual, not the community, is the basic unit of human life. Society is based therefore on a contract, not a covenant—an agreement, not a basic relationship. The objective of this contract is to promote such interests as individuals have in common and to secure their freedom to express themselves as they will, consistent with the right of others to do the same.

There is a contradiction in this philosophy, which has built itself into Western, especially American, society from the time of John Locke, its eighteenth-century founder, to the present. Politically, it shows in the endless effort to define individual liberties over against the demands of responsibility, for family, neighborhood, school, society, or nation. Economically, it has produced the strange dogma that the market system based on the individual's search for greatest profit in production, sale, and finance will produce the greatest welfare for all. It has created the difficulty we have today in justifying public action to control the excesses of the private sphere for the common good. Personally, it is expressed in an ethos of self-gratification and material possession that flies in the face of the family values and the community loyalties in which we also believe. Individualist humanism has never stood on its own foundation. It has always assumed and depended on some community ethos to give it life, meaning, and direction.

In three quite different ways, the church has tried to provide this ethos.

First, the churches of the Reformation, especially the Puritans of New England, but also the Quakers, Baptists, and others in their ways, imparted to English-speaking North American society a sense of political community quite different from that of the European countries from which the colonists came. We have already described its quality. It was still a Christian society. Most of our ancestors arrived with their faith. Indeed, many of them were refugees from persecution because of their faith. They believed that their lives

and destiny were in God's hands. They tried to structure their new society accordingly. But at the heart of
this faith was a covenant and a mission, not a social
order. They did not expect the world to become a
Christian culture and certainly not the kingdom of
God. They knew about the temptations of wealth and
power, both in society and in the church. They expected
the continuing judgment of God on this and all other
sin. But they did believe that God is faithful and that
the promise of the gospel is for the whole of the common life. They set out, therefore, to form a secular
order whose justice, freedom, and human relations
might bear some witness to this promise.

As a result of this, the United States of America has
become a nation formed out of all its ethnic diversity by
that secular image of God's covenant, a Constitution,
that defines the political conditions of our life together.
Allegiance to this constitution, not language, culture, or
heritage, makes a citizen. On the one hand, it is a contract among the people, hammered out by negotiation
and compromise. On the other, it is a living process. It
is constantly being reinterpreted and occasionally
changed to include peoples who had been excluded:
African Americans who had come here as slaves;
indigenous peoples who were here before Europeans
arrived; women, to whom custom had long given a subordinate place; the poor who fall victim to our ruthless
economic system.

These struggles are still going on. The unity of the
nation is threatened, tested, and sometimes, by God's
grace, reformed by them. Insofar as the Constitution
provides a relative transcendence over the prejudices
of the moment and points us toward the deeper values

of our life together, it is an instrument of God. It is, with its reminder of God's covenant, a sign of hope and a possible instrument of change as we try to define justice more deeply and inclusively.

The danger in all of this is, of course, legalism. It is the sin with which Lutheran theologians reproach their Reformed sisters and brothers in the faith even today. That the United States is the most litigious society in the world today, that we continually try to define and enforce all human relations by law, is partly the heritage of a covenant theology insufficiently redeemed by Christ. The Constitution regulates, it does not create, political community. Its structure of rights and responsibilities, its legitimation of and its limits on human power, and its protection of the weak against the strong are all relative and depend too much on the fallible wisdom of public opinion and the Supreme Court. God's covenant reaches out beyond the Constitution just as it has inspired and undergirds it. What is just, what is liberating, what the structure of our responsibility to one another is in this political community we call America needs continually to be rediscovered in response to the presence, work, and calling of Christ among us all. This is the church's business, both in the structuring of its own life and in its prophetic witness, both by analysis and by action in the field of public policy.

It is not surprising, therefore, that a second strand of Christian life has woven its way into American history—the emphasis on religious experience as the heart of faith and the basis of community. In its eighteenth-century origins, among the Moravian Brethren in Germany, the

Methodists in Britain, and the American Great Awakening, it did not contradict the two-realms doctrine of Luther or the covenantal theology of the New England Puritans. Rather, it sought to deepen these with personal commitment to the reign of Christ, not only in the world but in the self and in the intimate community of the faithful. This was, insists H. Richard Niebuhr, writing about the American scene, first of all a matter not just of feeling, but of enlightenment and action.

> The kingdom of Christ was the liberty of those who had received some knowledge of the goodness of God, and who reflected in their lives the measure of their knowledge and devotion. The kingdom of Christ remains then a rule of knowledge. To be a member of this kingdom is to be one who sees the excellency and the beauty of God in Christ, and so loves him with all his heart for his own sake alone. Such knowledge requires activity. The kingdom of Christ is the kingdom of love, and love is not only an emotion; it is a tendency to action, or action itself (1956:105, 112).

The influence of this movement on American society has been powerful and in at least two ways profoundly paradoxical.

1. Its emphasis on individual decision, commitment, and action has produced a host of initiatives for mission, social service, and action, and at the same time a deep conservative conformity to the individualist status quo. From the beginning, this evangelical awakening was a movement of converted individuals and voluntary associations. Its followers assumed a

God-ordered world, but thought little about it. Politics was not their concern. Instead, their Christ-centered optimism led them to spread the model of their communities into the society around them. It was a model that inspired the African-American churches, whether slave or free, as well. They built schools and hospitals. They joined and inspired humanitarian causes of all kinds—for temperance, peace, prison reform, or struggles to free slaves or alleviate poverty. On the western frontier, Methodist and Baptist preachers followed the pioneers, converting drunks and outlaws, and making their congregations centers of new community life. Once again Niebuhr puts it eloquently:

> They knew the fallacies present in the dogmas of natural liberty and human goodness, but they also knew that man was not destined to live in ignorance, and under restraint. They had confidence in the promise that God would write his laws upon the inward parts and make men (and women) fit for liberty, and they knew God was doing it now. Hence they were not afraid of freedom as the traditionalists were…. They did not contend for it save as their contact with the underprivileged made them partisans, or as their opposition to the hopeless reign of restrictive law made them allies of the humanist democrats, or as their love for the creatures of God bade them seek the equal rights of all. They followed their own line of attack, preaching the kingdom of Christian liberty, the conversion of minds and hearts to the love of God and of man in God. They pursued the ultimate and permanent revolution, the complete liberty of man in a community of

love. Because they did so, the struggles for a limited liberty profited. In America, as in England,
the Christian enlightenment stood beside the
rational enlightenment in the battle for democracy, and it furnished ten soldiers, to the cause
where the latter furnished one, for it dealt with
the common men (and women) about whom the
rationalists wrote books (1956:124).

This is a true picture, but it is only part of the story.
As the nineteenth and twentieth centuries have pro-
gressed, this image of converted individuals in voluntary community has become itself a social ideology. Its
relation to society as a whole is at best paradoxical. On
the one hand, the distinction between the saved community and the lost world has been greatly strengthened. The aim of evangelism has become to rescue
people from the world—usually understood as their
own personal sins and temptations, along with the
institutions that cater to them (saloon, brothel, gam-
bling den, etc.)—into personal union with Christ. Like
the Radical Reformers, the only community, the only
culture that matters, is that of the believers. Unlike the
Radical Reformers, this community is built less on the
discipline of discipleship than on the experience of
being saved and the emotional bond of those who have
gone through this experience. The converted are no
longer sinners. Their sin has been washed away by the
sacrifice of Christ. Revival meetings remind them of
this by repeating the experience. They become a cultural ritual that pulls the community together and may
bring others into it.

On the other hand, the saved community reaches
out into the world through saved individuals, who by

their piety and character spread goodness and love. They may do so by personal acts of sympathy or service, through charitable institutions, or by the way they run businesses or dispense philanthropy. By these ministries, voluntary and grounded in individual motivation and choice, the world is made a better place. The church is the source of inspiration for this, but it plays no direct role, except in matters of personal morality. Gradually then, the Christian liberty of sinners saved by Christ and the natural liberty espoused by humanists blend in harmony. Christian faith becomes one private experience among others in a humanist cultural milieu that honors benevolence but believes in free enterprise, competition, and natural selection. In a curious paradox, it sanctifies this culture by its own spiritual individualism while professing to transcend it. The "Christian Coalition" is only the latest example.

One should not underestimate this movement at its best. Much of what Niebuhr described in the eighteenth century has continued into the twentieth. Passionate personal conversion in group experiences led to the world missionary enterprise in nineteenth-century Britain and America. A whole ethos of voluntary service groups devoted to meeting human need and reforming human character—from the YM/YWCA to the Salvation Army, from the temperance movement to world relief—has been energized by its experience-based piety. Missing, however, is the objectivity of the body of Christ as the basis for human community, and the gospel of Christ's reign as judgment and grace for the nations and cultures of the world. Missing is repentance and humility among born-again Christians for

their continuing bias, their cultural pride, and their
worship of power and success. Where faith is based in
individual experience and expressed in gathered communities of those who share it, doors are closed to a
word of God through the church for other communities in other cultures. The whole problem of gospel and
community is bypassed; one culture-bound solution is
imposed as the Christian way. It is a solution that con-
stricts the very promise of God for the peoples of the
world, which the Christian convert is called to proclaim. Therefore, as these missions have spread their
experience-based message and culture across the
world, they have won a few, but have alienated many.
We desperately need to recover the union of personal
conversion with covenant community that Niebuhr
discerned in the early years of our history.

2. This movement's belief in conversion as a personal experience, its evangelical zeal, and its uncritical
use of dogma and Scripture have both united the community of believers and divided it. There is no doubt
that the earliest converts to these experience-centered
communities intended, not to divide the church, but to
inspire it with new enthusiasm and energy. In large
measure they did so. Moravian Brethren in Germany
and Wesleyan class meetings in England thought of
themselves as special communities within the Lutheran
or Anglican churches where they arose. It was church
members whom they tried to awaken to new levels of
commitment and send out as evangelists and missionaries. In North America, ecclesiastical conditions were
different, but the intention was the same. This spirit
infected all denominations and, faced with a fragmented body of Christ, projected its own ecumenical

and missionary vision, and developed its own organizations and sometimes its own denominations as well. But still the object of these awakened enthusiasts was to arouse all Christians—the whole community of believers, however organized—to new life and mission toward the conversion of an unbelieving world.

Sometimes the churches resisted them, and division resulted. Many American communities are studded even today with two congregations of the same denomination on the same street that split in the nineteenth century because one became impatient with the emotional reserve of the other. The first groups of theological students committed to foreign mission at Andover and Princeton were secret societies, for fear of disapproval from professors and church authorities. Yet the churches often supported the initiatives of the enthusiasts as well. The first missionary society, the American Board of Commissioners for Foreign Mission, was nondenominational but was supported by many denominations. Not only revival preachers, but the Sunday School Union, the YMCA, the Salvation Army, the Student Volunteer Movement, and many other evangelical enterprises worked through congregations, drew on church members, and supplemented the ministry of the churches while inspiring them to evangelistic outreach. In a paradoxical turn of history, the apostolic reality of the one body of Christ in mission to the world, broken by forces more social than theological into denominational fragments, was replaced by the vision of a vast association of converted individuals, united by their common experience of being saved, and the desire to share it with others.

It was an exhilarating vision, as the words and lives of its adherents testify. But it could not carry the weight of the gospel in the long run. Human experience, even the experience of God's saving love, is still human and therefore limited by the life and customs of one culture. The evangelical movement of nineteenth-century America therefore could go only in one of two directions. One was toward participation in the wider and deeper mission of the ecumenical movement, for which its spirit had helped open the way. Of this we will speak below. The other was toward an orthodoxy by which true conversion could be distinguished from false, and the certainty of faith maintained even against other Christians. This search for orthodoxy has taken several paths, and each has produced a new division in the community of believers.

a. The most common is that of doctrine and biblical interpretation. It has led to a strange marriage. Fundamentalism—that is, the founding of Christian faith on certain words and statements of Scripture and the propositions derived therefrom—is foreign to the evangelical spirit. But when faith is grounded in personal experience alone, it needs further assurance. The fear that underlies the search for it is real; humanism is always a threat, and a temptation. The doctrine then becomes the community's protection and its bulwark, even against other Christians whose experience is different and whose faith is more free.

b. Another path leads into greater intensity, and therefore greater assurance, of the experience itself. In Pentecostalism, the Spirit supplements, even replaces at times, the experience of salvation in Christ. The congregation is bound more closely together, not by external assurance, but by the intensity, the ecstasy, of the experience itself. Outsiders, even other Christians, are excluded, not by a barrier of doctrine, but because they cannot penetrate the heart of an experience that defines the community.

c. Still another way is that of apocalyptic expectation. God's plan of salvation, deduced from biblical texts and confirmed by signs, becomes the assurance that fortifies the saved community. The whole discussion among Christians about the reign of Christ and the meaning of Christian hope is here short-circuited by faith in the plan.

There are many others. Not all are new. Some are aberrations that have afflicted the church from its earliest days. Important for us is that they are proliferating in postmodern America, as membership in traditional churches declines, and that they are rooted in the experience-centered individualism that has both stimulated and distorted American Christianity for the past three centuries. As long as a basic covenantal ethos, rooted in the church's life and witness, pervaded our culture, this stimulus had a context and a counter-balance. Today, in a postmodern society where even secular individualism has been cut loose from the humanist faith that limited it and gave it meaning, everything depends on discovering the community-building work of Christ that will overcome and give new direction to our individual experience.

With this we turn, third, to the ecumenical witness of the church. The twentieth-century ecumenical movement did not come from church institutions as such. It arose out of the missionary experience of evangelical Christians, with all their strengths and weaknesses described above. As they met, on the western frontiers of the North American continent or in countries around the world, the question of their unity became ever more critical for the integrity of their mission. They were witnesses, after all, not to one experience of salvation but to one Savior and Lord for all peoples. So they banded together where they could, and called all Christians, of whatever confession, to join them. The Student Volunteer Movement for Foreign Mission was formed in 1886, and the World Student Christian Federation in 1895 moved by this impetus. Several world missionary conferences were held in the last half of the nineteenth century. The last of them, in New York in 1900, labeled itself for the first time, ecumenical. All of this was spiritual preparation for engaging the churches of the world, from Orthodox to Pentecostal, in a twentieth-century search for, and experience of, their unity in Christ and their mission to the communities of the world, both prophetic and redemptive.

This search defines the ecumenical movement. We are still engaged in it. It has two dimensions on the plane of this world: repentance and transformation.

Repentance has meant the searching, critical discovery, in encounter with other nations and societies, of the cultural bias and self-centered desires that we mix with the gospel, despite our best intentions, when we bring it to others. Slowly, and through many trials, we have learned how to rediscover the promise of God in the life and mission of churches in other lands, as judgment and correction to ourselves. Revolution, as in China, has driven missionaries out, and the church has found its own ways of community and mission, from which we can learn. Nationalism, as in India, has closed the door to Western leadership and funds, and the church has entered into the critical task of helping a many-cultured nation to define itself—in ways that may help Americans to understand the gospel better for our pluralistic society. But most important, the church ecumenical—through the World Council of Churches, the Vatican, various Catholic missionary orders, the evangelical Lausanne Movement for world mission, and other agencies—has brought churches from every continent together in reflection and action toward a church in mission to all the nations and cultures in the world. The church, in other words, is being transformed and rediscovered by encounter that brings together churches of radically different confessions, believers from cultures and classes strange and even antagonistic to each other, into a community of dialogue, transformation, and prayer.

The process is far from complete. Every encounter brings risk. New churches spring up every week outside the movement. The trend in large parts of the world is toward sectarian localism that ignores or rejects the one universal body of Christ. Some churches retreat from ecumenism into their nations or cultures. Others live in fear, in nations dominated by other faiths or ideologies. Still the ecumenical ferment continues. The realities that guide it are clear:

a. World community is, in the purpose of God and by the work of Christ in the Spirit, personal. It is neither a collection of individuals nor an order of reason and nature, but a reflection in human affairs of God's covenant, calling, and promise in Jesus Christ, which the church lives and proclaims. Laws and structures, economic or political, and organization and management are all secondary to this primary character. So are individual ambitions and liberties.

b. The gospel creates, renews, and inspires the variety of human cultures and secularizes them at the same time. They are blessed as expressions of human creativity and community, in their limited time and purpose. They are called to be open to change through encounter with other cultures and with history. In the words of Lamin Sanneh, "Christians hallow culture by the paradox of denying its intrinsic sacrality, and elevate it by opposing its idolization" (1993:138).

c. The gospel confronts all cultures, including "Christian" ones, with the call to continual repentance and reform in the light of God's purpose for them, to realize justice, to reflect in the creative turmoil of this age some image of the love that has come to the world in Christ, and to live toward that final economy when in the fullness of time all things will come to completion in him.

The questions these guidelines pose are clear as well. They are ecumenical questions. They are also American.

*How can the world find peace in some structured agreement among the nations, while allowing cultures, ways of life, and even languages to flourish, compete, and change each other? What is the relation between this secular enterprise and the church's witness?*

It is the business of the Christian church in mission to legitimate, to criticize, and to personalize government as an instrument of peace and justice among the cultures and nations of the world, including, of course, America. Our Constitution still holds us together. It is a secular covenant among the people, the cultures, and the interest groups of this society. But if this covenant is not continually subjected to the inspiration and the critical judgment of God's covenant that Christian believers recognize and proclaim, it will break down into a contract among the strong and the rich to pursue their welfare at the cost of the weak and the poor. This is happening in America today. Government agencies of public welfare, environmental protection, regulation of science, commerce, and industry for the public good, and protection for the disadvantaged are being attacked, dismantled, and underfunded. Christians are called on now more than ever to uphold, renew, and deepen the secular basis of community by legitimating government theologically for its God-ordained task of curbing private interests and serving public justice and peace.

The other side of this political task is to bring the resources of God's history with the covenant people to bear on defining and promoting justice in the public realm. The struggle to do this goes on continually as interest groups compete with one another to influence law and government policies. Christians are part of these groups, with all their divisions of race, income, worldview, and region. But they are more. As believers and members of the church, they respond to the work of a God whose peace reaches out to reconcile races and cultures with one another in Christ and to make covenant also with the stranger, the poor, the defenseless, and the weak. Christians are servants of this justice, especially when it means risking our own political security and compromising our own material well-being to bring it about. It is a secular enterprise. It demands careful analysis of the way human interests work in a sinful world. It involves both struggle, compromise, and openness to judgment and corrections if our actions are wrong. The way we so live and act is a witness to the gospel.

*How can the church express the community of humankind, and indeed of all creation, that is given in Christ, and at the same time cultivate and rejoice in the diversity of cultures and languages, of nations with their various structures, values, and ways of life?*

In the great vision that concludes the Bible, the Triune God penetrates all nations, cultures, peoples, and enterprises on the earth, blesses and transforms them, and brings all the fruits of their diverse creativity into one community whose light is the glory of God and whose lamp is the Lamb, the crucified and risen Christ. "By its light shall the nations walk; and the kings of the earth shall bring their glory into it.... They shall bring into it the glory and honor of the nations" (Rev. 21:24, 26).

The churches in our cultures have been faithful to this witness only in part. Despite the Puritan vision that formed our Constitution and the experience of salvation that inspired so much of our nineteenth-century faith and mission, churches in the United States have, over the years, been the main vehicles of the cultural self-consciousness of the immigrant minorities who have made this country their home. This is true of us all, even the Dutch, the Germans, and the Anglo-Saxons, who first settled among the people whom they called "Indians," and created the culture of early America. There is spiritual strength in this; there are also problems. For example:

a. African-American churches have given faith, hope, identity, and culture to an oppressed people struggling for freedom. What is today the mission of still segregated churches, black and white, in realizing a community in Christ that will at the same time honor and support African-American culture and leadership in society?

b. Roman Catholic churches gave dignity and solidarity to Irish, Italian, and many other European minorities that were the despised lower classes of our nineteenth-century cities. Today these people are distinguishable only by their religion, not their culture. But Hispanic Americans are entering the United States in such large numbers that there is talk of a bilingual if not bicultural American society. Most are nominally Roman Catholic, but many have left that church, a few to become Protestant, but most to form independent, often Pentecostal Christian communities whose vital spirituality baffles Catholics and Protestants alike. Which way lies community in this plurality, whether Christian or secular?

c. Among Asian immigrants, Koreans pose a special challenge. They are strongly Protestant Christian, with a minority Roman Catholic or Pentecostal. Their cultural coherence is strong and usually church based. Many become Christians when they immigrate. Their churches are often aggressively evangelistic. They may become part of American denominations, but cultural separation remains.

Churches also participate, through their cultural segregation, in the class divisions of American society: by residence (rural, urban, and suburban); by work (industrial, menial, managerial, and professional); by education; and most of all, by income. Subcultures grow up around these divisions—of affluence, of poverty, of establishment, and of alienation. Conscience drives many projects of charity and service that cross these lines—soup kitchens, clothing drives, housing construction, and the like—but this movement from above to below does not itself liberate or empower. It does not create community among equals that would bear witness to the one word of God. We are still learning how to break down the barrier between privilege and insecurity, between contentment and need.

*How can the Christian community involve itself in the formation and renewal of cultures in many human communities while at the same time discerning how God's judgment and transforming grace operate in each of them?*

Here the ecumenical question takes a new form for us. How can we deepen Christian community across class and cultural lines? How can the churches, in our segregated cultures, inspire community in the changing ethos of secular American culture today? How can we define together the form of the gospel for our society? In a world fragmented by broken families and neighborhoods, driven by individualism and competition, always threatened by conflict where one group's welfare impinges on another, to answer these questions with our lives is a critical Christian ministry. It is not easy. On the one hand, the church has been separated not only from the state but from public life as well. It has been privatized and marginalized, consigned to a religious arena by a world that pays no attention to the public claim of Christ. On the other hand, the churches too often are tempted to prosper by absorbing the values and standards of the cultures around them into their methods and their message.

But the church in God's purpose transcends both of these. It is a social creation of the Spirit within human culture. It exists in the world as the new humanity which makes known the economy of God in creation, in redemption, and in the fulfillment of all things in Christ. It lives between the times as a foretaste and instrument of the good news of God's reign. Its ministry and its organization need to reflect and serve its role as a community that lives and fully participates in the society where it is, but with a different set of values and informed by a different hope.

How can a congregation in our cultures be this church? How far are the elements of it already there in its life, despite the sins described above? How far is a new spirit and structure required? One proposal suggests that our dilemma requires a radical separation. "The Church exists today as resident aliens, an adventurous colony in a society of unbelief.... The most creative social strategy we have to offer is the church. Here we show the world a manner of life the world can never achieve through social coercion or governmental action. We serve the world by showing it something it is not, namely, a place where God is forming a family out of strangers" (Hauerwas and Willimon 1989:49, 83). The church bears its witness to Christ's reign and promise for the world by *being* this community over against all the cultural and social realities that also claim our loyalties. Others, skeptical of the sectarianism this invites, seek a more corporate reformation and a more organized witness of the church to the world in all its creative and sinful variety. All agree, however, that there are certain signs of the Spirit's work. Let this chapter close with these signs:

1. *A missionary understanding of biblical revelation.* The Bible is the story of God's creation, judgment, and redemption of the world in all its diverse and competing cultures, nations, and powers. In the fading Christendom of our congregational awareness, we too often forget this. Then the gospel is individualized. Believers turn in upon themselves, their problems, and their immediate community. In truth, we are caught up in the history that began with God's covenant with the Hebrew people, found its center in Jesus Christ, and looks forward to the fulfillment of all things in him. This is our story. It saves us from ourselves and defines who we are. It blesses us in our many communities and subjects them and us to the judging and redeeming work of Christ, with whom we live in the church. It sends us into an unbelieving world to bring that world, with all its nations, into this covenant and this history as well. The word of God in Scripture illuminates the work of God in the world today and tomorrow among all peoples. This is how the church is called to study and respond to it.

2. *A community, both pastoral and prophetic.* Too often these are played off against each other. What is really at stake, however, is pastoral imagination out of

which prophecy grows. A congregation, of course, experiences and expresses God's compassion and reconciling love among its members. If it does not, it dies. But God's compassion is inclusive. It reaches out to the spiritual and physical suffering of people beyond the bounds of every culture-defined community. When pastoral care of the congregation goes this route, toward those who have been pushed to the margins of church and society, it moves toward prophecy as well. God's judgment on human oppression and injustice is the other side of God's steadfast love. The church's prophetic witness against social evil is not some abstract concern for a just order, but part of its witness to the crucified Christ, who took all our sins and suffering on himself and triumphed over them. If we can forge that link in the minds and hearts of believers, we will have made giant strides toward creating congregations in mission, whatever form they may take.

3. *A church, both congregational and ecumenical.* No community of Christians has a private line to God. The interaction between unity and plurality is central to the faithful life of every congregation, just as it is for the church catholic and ecumenical across the world. This is a double movement. Churches, especially local congregations, do and should penetrate the souls of neighborhoods, towns, cities, businesses, labor unions, ethnic groups, cultures, and nations as they bring the gospel to them. By that same gospel they are also called into dialogue and community with congregations from other neighborhoods, other cities, other cultures, and other places on the economic scale. They challenge each other. They call each other in the name

of God to repentance and reformation. They are enriched by each other's spirituality and insight. This is the meaning of the ecumenical movement as it takes form in the life of every local Christian community.

4. *A church, gathered and dispersed.* The Confession of 1967 of the Presbyterian Church (U.S.A.) is a good guide here:

> The church gathers to praise God, to hear his word for humankind, to baptize and to join in the Lord's Supper, to pray for and present the world to God in worship, to enjoy fellowship, to receive instruction, strength and comfort, to order and organize its own corporate life, to be tested, renewed and reformed, and to speak and act in the world's affairs as may be appropriate to the needs of the time.

> The church disperses to serve God wherever its members are, at work or play, in private or in the life of society. Their witness is the church's evangelism. Their daily action in the world is the church in mission to the world. The quality of their relation with other persons is the measure of the church's fidelity (Presbyterian Church [U.S.A.] 1991:9:36–37).

There is something wrong with the picture of a Christian congregation whose members gather on Sunday morning to worship God, to hear the Word, to share in fellowship, and then "come back from church" to take part, as Christian individuals, in secular life until it is time "to go to church" again next Sunday. In reality, we are members of the body of

Christ with our whole being. Our individuality is *in* that membership, not apart from it. Our task then is to understand the church as corporately present in and with all its members throughout the week, wherever they are at work or play, and to focus this plural ministry in the gathered life of the church. This might mean church members would analyze the societies in which they are engaged—family, school, workplace, politics, or elsewhere—so as to discern and respond to the work of Christ there, and sharing this ministry with the whole congregation for its counsel, support, and intercession. It could lead to church members developing a style of Christian presence as citizens in public life that would include critical involvement with social policies and structures, and bringing this practice too before the congregation for its participation and critique. It would certainly mean the congregation's developing a style of worship, of Bible study, and of education that corrects, informs, inspires, and supports all these secular ministries of its members and brings them into focus as plural witnesses to the one redeeming work of Christ.

In short, the oneness we are given in Christ challenges us at every point to discern how God's reconciliation of the world is working to weave society together despite all the self-centered conflicting structures of human life. The word *solidarity* is too crude to describe this mission. A fine sensitivity to new relationships, a careful awareness of the concerns of persons and groups whose social experience differs from our own, and the transformation of these relationships in the presence, proclaimed or hidden, of Christ is the ministry that is needed. The unity that blesses our pluralisms is not our creation, but God's.

# 3

# The Gospel,
# the Power of God, and Human Powers

But we proclaim Christ crucified, a stumbling block to Jews and folly to Gentiles, but to those who are called, both Jews and Greeks, Christ the power of God and the wisdom of God. For the foolishness of God is wiser than men, and the weakness of God is stronger than men.

For consider your call, brethren; not many of you were wise according to worldly standards, not many were powerful, not many were of noble birth; but God chose what is foolish in the world to shame the wise, God chose what is weak in the world to shame the strong, God chose what is low and despised in the world, even things that are not, to bring to nothing things that are, so that no human being might boast in the presence of God (1 Cor. 1:23–29).

This paradox is at the heart of Christian faith. It is the good news that Christians live by and proclaim. It has also been unrealistic nonsense to much the world and downright offensive to part of it, from the time the incarnate Christ first embodied it. Once again, Pontius Pilate's conversation in the Praetorium with an enigmatic Jesus makes the point. "Pilate therefore said to him, 'You will not speak to me? Do you not know that I have power to release you, and power to crucify you?' Jesus answered him, 'You would have no power over me unless it had been given you from above'" (John 19:10–11). The miscommunication was total. Pilate gave up on the interview and tried to handle the situation with his own resources. Indeed, he had the power. But he was also surrounded by other powers that coerced him: the power of the mob crying for Jesus' blood, the power of the chief priests who demanded Jesus' death on the basis of their law, and ultimately, the power of Caesar with whose disfavor the crowd and the priests threatened him. In the end he made the decision to crucify an innocent man in order to keep the peace, but he did so reluctantly, as if afraid to use the power given him. No power, not even Caesar, not even the gods of his pantheon, could take the burden of that decision from him.

It is a story for every age; but today it is the story of everyman and everywoman. Never has so much power of choice been at the fingertips of so many people: choices in the marketplace, choices of residence and community, choices in politics, choices of career, choices of self-expression, choices of procreation and family, and choices of recreation and leisure. All these choices impinge on the environment or other people. Our power of choice confronts theirs when interests clash. At the same time we are more the objects, and sometimes the victims, of the power of others than ever before. Wealthy titans wrestle for control of vast financial empires while workers, depositors, consumers, and even stockholders can only watch. Cultures are overridden by mass media and globalized economy. Job markets shift according to the demands of profitability and technological change, bringing wealth to some, poverty and homelessness to others. Yet even those who manage and control these enterprises consider themselves driven by forces they do not control—bound, like Pilate, by the necessities of their own power. What, then, is power? What does the crucified Christ have to do with it? How is the power of the Triune God related to the powers in human society, then and now?

### Power, the Powers, and the Covenant

What is power? As first witness we call the seventeenth-century philosopher Thomas Hobbes, whose view of things from the center of sinful humanity was uncompromising: "I put for a generall inclination of all mankind, a perpetuall and restless desire of Power after power that ceaseth only in Death" (1914:49; chap. 11). It is an insatiable appetite, of individuals and societies, he claimed. No one can be content with moderate power, for the enjoyment of it can never be secure. One must continually strive to protect it by acquiring more and more. Driven both by ambition and fear, the lust to expand power has no limits.

Hobbes was a dissenter in his age, but he was not alone. His somber realism sounded an undertone through the liberal humanist culture of the centuries that followed until, in the power struggles of the twentieth century, theologian Reinhold Niebuhr picked it up:

> Every group, as every individual, has expansive desires which are rooted in the instinct of survival

and soon extend beyond it. The will-to-live becomes the will-to-power. Only rarely does nature provide armors of defense that cannot be transmuted into instruments of aggression. Thus society is in a perpetual state of war. Lacking moral and rational resources to organize its life, without resort to coercion, except in the most immediate and intimate social groups, men remain victims of the individuals, classes and nations by whose force a momentary coerced unity is achieved and further conflicts are as certainly created (1947:18).

Perhaps this is a fair description of society in any age since the fall of Adam and Eve. It certainly describes the Near Eastern world in which Israel arose during the first millennium before Christ. It was a world of small nations, each with its god and its king, each trying, by war or other means, to expand its power at the expense of the other while dealing as best they could with the imperial power of Egypt on the west and later Assyria or Babylon on the east. Sometimes these kings annihilated their enemies; sometimes they made covenants with them—often to avoid destruction— whereby two peoples became one community, with one god. The central reality in all of this was power. The gods they worshiped were the guarantors of this power. They were gods who fought with their people, who brought them victory in war and prosperity in peace. If they did not, they were destroyed with their people, and the gods of the victors took over.

This is the world in which the God of Abraham, Isaac, and Jacob intervened to choose, call, and make covenant with the people of the Hebrews. So began a history that redefined the relation between human power in a fallen world and the power of God.

God did this—not one of the deities thrown up by the religious and political needs of one nation or another; not the mythological pantheon that sanctified the cosmic order of a great empire, but the maker of the heavens and the earth. God chose and called.

The people came into existence as they responded to One whom they symbolized in human words but whom they could not name, for naming would mean control; it would mean ordering into a human world. The God to whom the Hebrews gave the cryptic name Yahweh was lord of the relationship. This lord could—and can—be known only *in* the encounter, *in* the history of this relationship, to which the people give themselves in trust and hope. God created the covenant people, with all the quality of common life, all the calling, and all the promise by which they live and to which they are brought back when they go astray. The people did not create God. This is the difference between God and an idol.

In the history of this revealed relationship, the people come to know God not in the sense of information about, but as insight into the character of the One who knows them and guides their destiny. That God is almighty, there is no doubt. The Bible is filled with celebrations of divine power, over enemies and idols in this world and as creator of the heavens and the earth, lord of the floods and the tempests, ruler of the nations. But God's power is not abstract omnipotence; it is self-limited by God's own character. In Karl Barth's words: "God's freedom is not merely unlimited possibility or formal majesty and omnipotence, that is to say empty, naked sovereignty. God himself, if conceived of as unconditional power, would be a demon and as such his own prisoner. In the light of his revelation, God is free in word and deed; he is the source and measure of all freedom, insofar as he is the lord, choosing and determining himself first of all... to be the Father and the Son in the unity of the Spirit.... Only in this relational freedom is God sovereign, almighty, the lord of all" (1960:71–72).

God *is* the God of the covenant. *In* the justice and mercy that casts down the proud, that reaches out to save and establish the poor and the powerless, and *in* faithfulness to an unfaithful people, God is God. The power of God to reign, to judge, to save, and to fulfill is covenantal.

What has happened here in the history of the Jews, as also in the crucifixion, resurrection, and the coming reign of Christ, is the secularizing, the historicizing, and the humanizing of power by the self-revealing action of God. The nation of Israel was not called to be powerful in the world struggle for survival and dominance, but to bear witness in all its life to the sovereign power of the covenant Lord who had chosen them. This power secularized all the other powers. God created the heavens and the earth, and governed human affairs. There was no other sacred force to be worshiped or feared. In this context the children of Israel became the bearers of the promise of God for a future of peace whose full dimensions could be discovered only as the people explored the goodness and steadfast love of God's own character. It was the beginning of history and hope beyond victory in battle. It opened a dimension of humanity that was finally revealed in Christ.

The Hebrew people wrestled with this God and with this calling throughout their history. In the early books of the Bible, especially in the story of the conquest of Canaan, there is much that reflects the pagan view around them of a tribal god who destroys enemies in battle; yet in this same story, the command to trust and obey the God of the covenant only was absolute. God, not human power, dominates events. The people demanded a king to unify the nation and to supplement divine power. They celebrated the royal priesthood of David. But most of the kings they were given divided the nation and, in the words of the historians, "did what was evil in the sight of the Lord." The nation prospered at times and made room in its temples for gods of wealth and good fortune alongside the Lord—only to hear the prophets, in the name of the Lord, denounce them for idolatry, for pride in their own strength and alliances, for greed, and for ignoring the plight of the poor. Finally, the people were defeated in war and driven into exile, while their prophets made known to them that this was the judgment of God on their rebellion and unfaithfulness to the covenant.

Yet all of this took place within the faithfulness, the steadfast love, of God toward the Hebrew people in calling, covenant, and promise. In the words of the psalm:

> The LORD works vindication
>     and justice for all who are oppressed.
> He made known his ways to Moses,
>     his acts to the people of Israel.

The LORD is merciful and gracious,
> slow to anger and abounding in steadfast love.
He will not always chide,
> nor will he keep his anger for ever.
He does not deal with us according to our sins,
> nor requite us according to our iniquities.
For as the heavens are high above the earth,
so great is his steadfast love toward those who fear him;
as far as the east is from the west,
> so far does he remove our transgressions from us.
(Ps. 103:6–12)

What, then, is the relation between this covenant power of God and the human power by which a society tries to secure itself in prosperity and peace, and expand itself in wealth and war? The highest prophetic insights only drove the paradox deeper. There were promises of a new covenant, written on the hearts of the people (Jer. 31:31–34); of a new radiance going out from Zion to establish law and peace among the nations (Mic. 4:1–4); and of Israel, the suffering servant, bearing witness to all the peoples of the redeeming power of the Lord of creation (Isa. 42–53). But these are prophetic visions, inspired by the God of the covenant, projected onto the power struggles of the world. They look forward to—indeed, they cry out for—the ultimate confrontation of the power of God with the powers of the world in the life, death, and resurrection of Christ.

The confrontation began even before Jesus was born, in the words of Mary's Magnificat: "(God) has shown strength with his arm, he has scattered the proud in the imagination of their hearts, he has put down the mighty from their thrones, and exalted those of low degree; he has filled the hungry with good things, and the rich he has sent empty away" (Luke 1:51–53). It was reflected in the events surrounding the birth: angels singing glory to God and telling shepherds to find the savior of the world in a stable in Bethlehem; wise men innocently threatening Herod with the question, "Where is he who has been born king of the Jews?" (Matt. 2:2). According to Mark's Gospel, at the beginning of his ministry "Jesus came into Galilee, preaching the gospel of God, and saying, 'The time is fulfilled, and the kingdom of God is at hand; repent, and believe in the gospel'" (1:14–15). Yet this proclaimer of God's reign used only the power of teaching and healing in his ministry. He denounced the religious authorities, aimed pointed barbs at the economically successful, and ignored, as far as he could, the political powers, both Roman and revolutionary. His parables of the kingdom warned of judgment to come but spoke far more of the new reality already at work in human life. He recruited his disciples from people of no special status and taught them to be servants like himself. Finally, he did not fight the powers that condemned him, but died, forgiving them, on the cross. The admonition in Paul's letter to the Philippians sums it up: "Have this mind among yourselves, which you have in Christ Jesus, who, though he was in the form of God, did not count equality with God a thing to be grasped, but emptied himself, taking the form of a servant, being born in the likeness of men. And being found in human form he humbled himself and became obedient unto death, even death on a cross" (2:5–8).

Then the text goes on: "Therefore God has highly exalted him and bestowed on him the name which is above every name, that at the name of Jesus every knee should bow, in heaven and on earth and under the earth, and every tongue confess that Jesus Christ is lord, to the glory of God the Father" (2:9–11). The power of God is the power to cancel the consequences of human sin, to justify and sanctify the sinner, to make human beings new in Christ. It is the power of the new reality present now in the risen Christ, to be fulfilled in the age to come.

Meanwhile, much is said in the New Testament about other powers and authorities. They are super-human; they are "in the air," somewhere between heaven and earth. Yet they are rooted in human activity and take form in human institutions. The one mentioned specifically is government (Rom. 13:1). But Mammon, the power of economic activity, could be another (Matt. 6:24); and Colossians speaks of "elemental spirits of the universe," which are similar: "philosophy and empty deceit, according to human tradition" (2:8). Could this mean ideology, or laws and customs that demand conformity by pressure of public opinion? The categories could be expanded. There are many of them, then and now. About them all, in New Testament perspective, certain things can be said.

a. They are powers created by God. They have their authority, their value, and their meaning in God's purpose and plan. They were created "through (Christ) and for him. He is before all things and in him all things hold together" (Col. 1:16).

b. They seek to follow their own direction and seek their own sufficiency apart from, and at times in rebellion against, God (Eph. 6:12). They are rooted in human desires, ambitions, and activities, in human idolatries and false absolutes. Their power comes partly from the human will, yet they develop structures and directions of their own that subject human beings and enslave them. In this sense they are indeed superhuman and demonic (Eph. 2:1-3).

c. Christ in creation was the origin and meaning of the powers. In his crucifixion he was their victim. In his resurrection he reigns over them. In this age and in the age to come he will triumph over them and "unite all things in him, things in heaven and things on earth" (Eph. 1:10; Cor. 15:24; Col. 2:15).

d. Human beings are caught up in this conflict between God and rebellious power, because they are themselves the battleground. God's power is here also *in* the covenant. The basic experience of the believer is to be forgiven, liberated from sinful self by the sacrifice of Christ, and empowered by the calling and the promise of new life in him. Another way of putting it is that men and women are called to be holy, to enter into communion with God the Holy Spirit. But divine holiness, being an expression of divine power, becomes a destructive threat to each of them, when they try to grasp power from self or world as center, apart from the relationship with God and neighbor that is given in Christ. "Do you not know that you are God's temple and that God's Spirit dwells in you? If any one destroys God's temple, God will destroy him. For God's temple is holy, and that temple you are" (1 Cor. 3:16–17). Holiness, the Holy Spirit, is the internal limit and direction that empowers human life. It is the inexorable judgment of God on our use of power that is in any way untrue to the promise and direction of God's covenant life in Christ.

Christians are witnesses to this power and stewards of its mysteries. They are witnesses first to the way in which the power of the Triune God judges and transforms them in their pursuit of what they believe to be just and good. They are continually learning repentance and experiencing forgiveness as they rediscover the ways by which God's love overrules human efforts to set up other absolutes and other hopes than those of the divine economy. They are stewards of the mysteries of this everlastingly dynamic justice, never masters but explorers as they prepare the way in this age for the coming of Christ. In a world dominated by the powers, knowing Christ's victory and coming reign over them, this means that Christians are to withstand these powers with "the whole armor of God" (Eph. 6:11), respect them in their proper function and limits (Rom. 13:1–9), and at the same time to bear witness to them of their place in "the manifold wisdom" of the economy of God to unite all things in Christ (Eph. 3:10).

## Gospel, Power, and the Powers Today

This is not the place to chronicle the shifts and changes among the powers that took place in more than a millennium of a civilization, which claimed to have heard and given form to the claim and promise of Christ. It is enough to say that built into that civilzation was a deliberate distinction, even a separation, of powers, based on awareness that those of this world can be blessed in their functions, but that they cannot justify and sanctify themselves. The church, on the other hand, embodied the judging and redeeming power of God in Christ among the powers of the world, but it could not, for that very reason, become one of those powers. For centuries, this interaction was played out in various ways, from the extreme separation of some monastics and Reformation radicals to the near synthesis of some Orthodox cultures. It still continues, as we have seen above, in cultures where the church and its faith are honored by the world in some degree as moral and spiritual authorities. It was the early breakdown of this interaction that produced the—still theological—cynicism of Thomas Hobbes's effort to redefine both divine and human power.

The world today, however, sees power quite differently. Almost from the beginning of time, human beings have assumed, despite their dreams of glory, that human power is limited. The forces of what we now call nature were to be feared because they could not be controlled. They were part of that superhuman reality in which the gods were involved, who might be petitioned and cajoled but never managed or coerced. The struggle for power was therefore a matter of competition, warfare, and control between human beings in their tribal or national solidarities for land and for political and cultural dominance. The gods might be called on to help, often in the hope that they could use the forces of nature to favor one nation or another, but the issue, up to the time of Thomas Hobbes at least, was human power over other human beings, challenged, and by God's grace sometimes modified, by the gospel of the crucified and risen Christ.

What has changed this whole perspective is the vast expansion of human power over nature itself. The conversion of fossil fuels, and more recently of the forces inside the atom, into controlled energy to drive machines has changed the very meaning of the word in the popular mind. It has come to mean a natural force to be harnessed for the satisfaction of human needs and desires. It becomes, then, a source to be channeled and tapped to expand the material possibilities of human life almost without limit. Human community is relevant only as people compete or cooperate to generate this power. They all, presumably, have the same access and the same parallel desires.

The relation of this explosion of human scientific knowledge and technological power to the Christian faith and message has been at best ambivalent. On the one hand, J. Lesslie Newbigin is right in discerning a new paganism in the Euro-American society that once was Christendom. Two ideologies have fought to define it.

The first is the humanist rationalism that we described in Chapter 1. It is rooted in confidence (1) that the human mind, using the methods of scientific investigation and technological invention, can plan and manage nature for human benefit without measurable limit; (2) that self-interested reason will control all misuse of power; and (3) that individual choices in the marketplace will lead naturally to general prosperity through free competition. God is at best a symbolic expression of the reason, goodness, and power of humanity realizing its future in a world of endless progress. The endless expansion of individual freedom and power, through control of the forces of nature, is the meaning of life. Covenantal relations, set forth in the faithfulness of God and the sacrifice of Christ, are at best a matter of private choice; at worst, obstructions to security and progress. This rationalism has organized the world during the past two centuries. Some societies have resisted, but none has been left unchanged by it. The scientific, technological, and economic structures this rationalism has created are the principal powers at work in our global society everywhere, even when those who wield and serve these powers no longer believe in the ideology that undergirds them.

The other ideology has challenged this humanism from within, with devastating consequences over the past century and a half. It was Karl Marx who first analyzed effectively the way in which the human will to power and profit destroys society, dehumanizes its members, and builds a system that cries out to be overturned by revolution from below. Marx shared the humanist confidence in human goodness and power. Indeed, he was more Promethean in his belief in the power of human labor in all its forms to remold nature to reflect human desires than most liberals. But his basic experience and conviction was that the system of production based on accumulation and investment of capital had alienated people from true control over the fruits of their own labor and had made most of them victims of a dynamic process that led to ever deeper impoverishment and dehumanization. Power struggle against the system—and against all the social and political institutions that uphold it—was for him a basic assertion of humanity.

Marx was more explicitly atheistic than his liberal humanist opponents because he discerned the hypocrisy of so much religion, which had made its peace with bourgeois power. He believed to the full in the inevitability and goodness of global industrialization, finance, technology, and science, but only when private control by an ever fewer elite would be replaced by the control of all the people, who have been schooled in a spirit of solidarity and freedom from private greed and individual desire by their experience of deprivation. The fact that this collectivist humanism failed in its most militant form does not diminish its power as a vehicle of collective action even today, whenever hope, among the deprived victims of the dominant powers in our world, wins out over cynicism and despair. Marxism failed as a humanist ideology. It remains a penetrating analysis of the way in which human avarice and greed are transmuted into the principalities and powers that work in the economic sphere. The paradox of Marxist economics that brings it close to Christian understanding is its combination of an objective science of economic forces in a sinful world with an implicit faith that these forces, because they destroy humanity, will bring judgment on themselves.

Two ideologies are here in a power struggle. Both replaced God with true humanity, and Christ with human planners as agents of salvation. Both try to bring in the kingdom by human power.

But this is only half the story. There is a more than human power in the dynamics of the scientific-technological revolution, despite the humanist pride of its agents. To put it bluntly, neither would have been possible had not the gospel been proclaimed and confessed in the world in which they arose. We have seen this in Chapter 1, as it affects the question of truth. It is equally true of power. Arend van Leeuwen expressed it a generation ago in his provocative book *Christianity in World History* (1964: chaps. II and III). It is the biblical revelation of the living God that first challenged every sacred structure of human thought and power with a calling to the people of God to pursue a secular, historical promise. The discovery that nature is created, and not in itself a realm of sacred spirits or deities or an eternal order of being, spurred scientists to explore its secrets and use them for human ends. The discovery that the dynamic center of reality and the moving force of history is the power of God in the risen Christ led to an exuberant exercise of free responsibility by believers. Its charter is in the New Testament itself in the words of the apostle Paul. We have heard it before in this book, but it bears repeating.

> This is how one should regard us, as servants of Christ and stewards of the mysteries of God.... To me, though I am the very least of all the saints, this grace was given, to preach to the nations the unsearchable riches of Christ, and to make all people see what is the economy of the mystery hidden for ages in God who created all things; that through the church the manifold wisdom of God might now be made known to the principalities and powers in the heavenly places. This was according to the eternal purpose which he has realized in Christ Jesus our Lord (1 Cor. 4:1; Eph. 3:8–11).

"Christianity," wrote the Russian Orthodox philosopher Nicholas Berdyaev, "had freed humanity from subjection to nature, and had set humans up spiritually in the center of the created world. Christianity alone inspired humanity with this anthropocentric feeling which became the fundamental motivating power of modern times. It made modern history with all its contradictions possible because it exalted humans above nature" (1936:117).

In doing so, it also exalted human beings above the principalities and powers in society—empires with their rulers, priests, and soldiers; families with their patriarchs and sometimes matriarchs; economic structures with their bankers, finance managers, and corporation CEOs; race, language, and culture groups with their prejudices—all of which hitherto had been clothed with an aura of authoritative power.

It was, in short, the Christian vision of human possibilities in Christ, embracing the whole range of existence and conquering the forces that held life in bondage, that empowered modern humanism with its basic inspiration and hope, whether free enterprise or socialist, whether individualist or collective. The spiritual and theological foundations of this vision have been replaced by humanist stilts; or, perhaps better, by wheels of human progress that need no foundations as long as they roll. But they are part of the history whose meaning and direction are given in the covenant of God in Jesus Christ for all the nations. They are among the powers being brought into the economy of God, of which Christians are stewards and witnesses. Christian and humanist themes have combined to inspire the greatest explosion of human power in history.

But the Christian church and its message have lost control of the process. First, as we have seen in the previous chapter, it was a loss of external power. Even before the ideology of free enterprise learned to dismiss it as irrelevant and counterproductive and the Marxists to denounce it as the people's opium, the practice of Christ's calling to servanthood and stewardship in the exercise of power in trade, business, and industry was quietly privatized. It became a matter of individual conscience, perhaps strengthened by the preacher's rhetoric, no longer an object of public policy and church discipline.

Second, the churches themselves fell into internal confusion about the relation between the covenant power of God and the expanding power of the industrial, scientific, and technological revolution in our age. Examples of this ambivalence abound. Let just one of them illustrate it—the missionary enterprise of the past two centuries.

There was no doubt about the primary motivation of this enterprise—to bring to all the world knowledge of the saving power of God and to make disciples of all peoples, individually or by nations and cultures. At the same time, these bearers of the gospel were not only part of the Western culture from which they came; to further their work, they also made use of the culture and the power it generated. William Carey went to India at the turn of the nineteenth century to bring, as he believed, both the gospel and the benefits of modern civilization. He became a scholar of Hindu culture in order to relate that culture to both. When John R. Mott called, in 1900, for the evangelization of the world in this generation, he saw all the powers of technology, commerce, and industry as God's servants to this end. His words were eloquent:

> Now steam and electricity have brought the world
> together. The Church of God is in the ascendant.
> She has within her control the power, the wealth,
> and the learning of the world. She is like a strong

and well-equipped army in the presence of the
foe. The only thing she needs is the Spirit of her
Leader and a willingness to obey his summons to
go forward. The victory may not be easy, but it is
sure (1911:130–31).

Missionaries did not in principle follow the flag of
their nations. But they went where they could and
used with gratitude the roads which political and economic power opened to them. Even the most pietistic
of them depended on the resources of this power and
projected it in their work. Educational, medical, and
social service mission work reinforced the positive con-
nection between the health, prosperity, and power of
Euro-American science, technology, and industrial
development, and the new life in Christ. Most
Christian missions were aware, of course, that the
gospel transcends and judges their own societies as
well. The call to foreign mission went with, and often
grew out of, the call to conversion and revival at home.
Missionaries in the field were often protectors of the
people they served against the colonial, military, or
economic power of the countries from which they
came. As, in this century, resistance to imperialism
grew to a tidal wave, many missionaries sided with
independence and even with revolutionary movements against the powers of their own Western society.
Twentieth-century missiological theory and missionary practice has been filled with efforts to redefine the
church's mission so as to express the judgment of God
on imperialist domination, whether political or economic, and to identify it with the true aspirations of
suppressed peoples everywhere.

The problem is, however, that these redefinitions have too often continued the ambivalence of our immediate ancestors about the relation between the covenant power of God in Christ, and human power. The power of an emerging nation, with its indigenous culture and politics, may balance and redirect the world powers of technology, weapons, and finance; but it is no less a human enterprise than they. Its faith is no less humanist, whatever its dominant religion may be. The power of the poor and oppressed may, if it can be effectively organized, force the managers of the world economy to compromise profit for greater justice, but this power is also human. There is no salvation in it.

What then is the relation between the power of the Holy Spirit at work in Christ for the reconciliation of the world, and the powers of political control, of economic globalization, or of human solidarities in nation or class in a technological world? This question has been a major theme of the twentieth-century ecumenical movement. Reinhold Niebuhr put it most sharply: "The problem of politics and economics is the problem of justice. The question of politics is how to coerce the anarchy of conflicting human interests into some kind of order, offering human beings the greatest possible opportunity for mutual support." The way to do this, says Niebuhr, is to balance power against power so as to neutralize the collective force of egoistic passion, to empower the powerless in the struggle, and to find techniques for harnessing its energy to social ends. All this is less than the ideal of love. "Yet the law of love is involved in all approximations of justice, not only as the source of the norms of justice, but as an ultimate perspective by which their limitations are discovered" (1979:81).

By the law of love, Niebuhr meant the self-sacrificing life and ministry of Jesus Christ which led to his death on the cross. He saw this as a transcendent yet ever-relevant presence in the world of human power struggles until the final judgment day. But is this the only role of Christ in the power struggles of our history? Dietrich Bonhoeffer, writing from prison in the last months of the Second World War, was more paradoxical and more positive. "Human religiosity," he wrote, "makes people look in their distress to the power of God in the world.... The Bible directs them to God's powerlessness and suffering; only a suffering God can help." Christ's ministry is not only one of love's perpetual judgment on the tenuous and relative justice achieved by managing the human power struggle. It is also the way by which the God of the Bible wins "power and space in the world by his weakness" (1972:361, inclusive language added by the author).

Building on such theologies as these and on the churches' soul-testing experience of betrayal and witness, of surrender and resistance, during the Nazi times and World War II, the World Council of Churches, in its Inaugural Assembly at Amsterdam in1948, posed the question afresh for Christians in the postwar world.

First, the Assembly was one of the earliest to recognize that "vast concentrations of power, which are under capitalism mainly economic and under communism mainly political," diminish the ability of men and women "to act as moral and accountable beings," and "that society, as a whole, dominated as it is by technics," is "more controlled by a momentum of its own than in previous periods." Control over nature is enhanced, but "destruction in war and social upheaval is increased by the uncontrolled forces it generates" (World Council of Churches 1948:190).

Second, the Assembly message made a ringing proclamation, echoing the Apostle Paul in Ephesians, of the victory of God in Christ over the powers of this world:

> There is a word of God for our world. It is that the world is in the hands of the living God, whose will for it is wholly good; that in Jesus Christ, his incarnate Word, who lived and died and rose from the dead, God has opened for everyone the gate of freedom and joy in the Holy Spirit; that the final judgment on all human history and on every human deed is the judgment of the merciful Christ; and that the end of history will be the triumph of his Kingdom, where alone we shall understand how much God has loved the world. This is God's unchanging word to the world. Millions of our fellow creatures have never heard it. As we are met from many lands, we pray God to stir up his whole Church to make this gospel known to the whole world, and to call on all people to believe in Christ, to live in his love and to hope for his coming (1948:Appendix).

We live, said the report of Section III, "in the light of that kingdom, with its judgment and mercy" with a certainty and a hope that no disorder of society can destroy, and "seek in every age to overcome the specific disorders which aggravate the perennial evil in human society" in assurance of the final victory that Christ will bring, over sin and death (1948:189).

Third, the report emphasizes that Christians and their churches have been involved in the very misuses of power and mistaken ideologies that drive the societies around them. They have "often given religious sanction to the special privileges of dominant classes, races and political groups. They have often concentrated on a purely spiritual or otherworldly or individualistic interpretation of their message and their responsibility. They have often failed to understand the forces which have shaped the society around them" (191). The church is therefore called to repentance and liberation from its own bondage to the powers of the world, as a part of its witness to Christ's victory.

Fourth, the authors of the report called for a style of social analysis and action that would respond to and point toward the power of God in Christ. They called it "responsible society." It meant, as Bonhoeffer had described it in "The Structure of Responsible Life" (1992:256–88, my trans.), living concretely for one's neighbor in the world of political and social powers, sharing problems, accepting the guilt of actions that are responsible but not pure, bearing witness in the human struggle to the judgment and mercy of Christ. It involved careful analysis of the powers of the world—technological development, political control, and social upheaval in both its communist and capitalist forms—in the effort to render them responsible to the human needs and hopes of those under their control, embodying that responsibility in structures of personal participation in decision making from below. It meant, in biblical terms, being stewards of the mysteries of the economy of God in the midst of the human economy, and witnesses to the powers in the world of their accountability to God and the people whose welfare they influence.

## The Gospel and Postmodern Power

In recent years the picture has changed. The ideologies of human power, both individualist and collectivist, both liberal and revolutionary, are in crisis. Most dramatic has been the breakdown of the communist command society, with its Marxist vision of a new humanity, in a classless society where all property is shared in common and the individual will to power is surrendered in service to the whole community. It was an ideal that could not control the powers of its world; it collapsed in its own corruption.

But Western society also, with its various combinations of market economy and social planning, faces powers with which its ideology cannot deal. Global investment, finance, and production operate by laws that create enormous wealth for a few but pay little attention to the welfare of noninvestors, workers, and the poor. For the time being, this global economy is flourishing; yet it is already beset by breakdowns for which the explanations, even after the fact, are never adequate. Meanwhile, parts of the globe are being changed for ages to come by exploitation of their resources. Our very technological progress accelerates the destruction of our environment, and no power, political or economic, can bring this process under control. Basically, economic progress is limited to certain nations and certain classes. The world as a whole is not developing toward prosperity, or even basic security, as was promised when the scientific-technological revolution began.

We can see the powers at work that are shaping our future. They are powers that we have cultivated. We are no longer sure they are under human control or are the bearers of human hope. Nor can we believe, if we ever did, that power will well up from the people— the poor and the oppressed—to give our whole techno- logical enterprise a humanizing direction. There is a great deal of resentment, anger, and rebellion abroad in the world. But its ideologies, and therefore its pow- ers, are fragmented and often set against each other by nation, by ethnic group, by race, and at times even by gender or sexual orientation.

Given this postideological confusion, this anxiety, and this cynicism, who are we as Christians? What is the form of our gospel for people confronted with human power in its superhuman forms today? Let this chapter close with a few suggested guidelines.

First, we are not primarily agents of human power, whether managerial, revolutionary, or even sacerdotal, to solve the moral problems of an unjust society. On the contrary, we are witnesses to the judging and transforming power of God in Jesus Christ. This power brings us, our neighbors, our social context, and the world to repentance. It liberates us all from our fears and our self-justifications, both personal and social. It directs each of us to our neighbors in love. We are not defenders of our securities, rights, and powers, but ser- vants of an economy that is not rooted or validated in human strategies, programs, or analyses, but plainly and simply in the victory of Christ over the powers of the world.

We have good news to proclaim, to enemies as well as to friends, to those who oppress us and to those who are our equals and likes. It is news of forgiveness and reconciliation offered to us all in Christ, so that we can repent and ask forgiveness of those whom we have offended and offer it to those who have offended us. It is news of rights and interests we can surrender for the sake of fruitful new relations with others, both one by one and in nations or cultures. It is news of sacrifices, personal and social, that echo in human society the sacrifice of Christ for us all. It is news of risks that can be taken with our immediate security, economic or political, in order to pursue the long-term common good, because the God of the covenant is Lord. This has all happened to us in Christ. It has happened for the world. It offers a new perspective on what power is.

Second, Christians are stewards of the mysteries of the power that has been given to us. We are called to deal responsibly and repentantly with it. This is, before God, a *secular* calling. It is our witness amid the conflicts and moral ambiguities of this age. Here is where the struggle against unjust powers, advocacy for the disadvantaged and for the public good, and defense of the environment against human depredation belong. Here is where we work for justice and integrity in the conduct of government, business, science, and technology.

This requires a careful, realistic analysis of the powers at work in society today unclouded by slogans or simplifications. It means seeking out and unmasking the ideologies with which special interests of all kinds rationalize their power, their status, or the activities they pursue. It means exposing the way power really works, above all the power of money, but also the power of information through the media, of political influence, and of organized groups of all kinds: religious, racial, ethnic, social, or economic. It calls for responsible engagement in the power struggle to work with the persons and forces there, both in criticism and in constructive proposals, toward directing the principalities of this world away from their own drive toward profit, control, and domination toward the service of justice, compassion, and the common good. It involves continual struggle, compromise, and new challenge to improve the level of justice and the depth of community in a sinful world of conflicting interests.

It also involves repentance. No exercise of human power, however responsible, is more than relatively just. Someone will be unjustly injured by any enterprise or by any solution to a social problem. Openness to correction for the social bias, the hidden self-interest, or the bald insensitivity that continually infects every use of power, however objective it claims to be, is at the heart of Christian stewardship. It is witness to the One who judges and forgives us all.

Third, we are witnesses that power is not only the self-expression of a subject, human or divine, not only control over things, but an ingredient of a relationship that also contains other elements. Impersonal powers are demonic. They lead one out of the covenant with God that gives life meaning and hope. This is hard to realize in a world where impersonal power is everywhere: in the forces of the market that govern production, sales, and finance; in the electricity that powers the machine on which these words are being written; in the software and the hardware of the machine itself; and even in the "personalized" mass communications we receive. We affirm these services. We are often grateful for their impersonality—that, for instance, this computer does not try to correct the theology as well as the spelling of what is written on it. But when services become themselves powers over our lives, their character changes. This is what happens unless the welfare of the community expressed in responsible public policy regulates and directs their activity.

Human power, therefore, including those dimensions which grow to superhuman proportions, has its constructive place as a servant of human relations as they flower in community. This is the criterion that should govern the policies of scientific research; technological invention, investment, and production; the government agencies that regulate and direct them; and all other decisions about the development and use of power in society. For example:

a. What is the right use of the power of government to limit, direct, regulate, and generally to make these powers responsible to the common good? Conversely, how much freedom must they have to be properly inventive and productive in improving the quality of human life ?

b. What balance should be struck between the exploitation of our natural environment for human benefit and the preservation of its ecosystem, in the stewardship of God's creation for this and future generations? What policies would assure this balance, and how can the political and economic powers of the world be coerced and induced to adopt them?

c. How can the creative diversity of cultures in the world be protected from and served by the power dynamics of the global system of mass media?

d. How can those who are affected by the decisions of these powers—laborers, consumers, the poor in this country or abroad, or the general public—be empowered to influence these decisions? How can impersonal power be brought under community control?

The church brings to all of these questions a freedom and a responsibility that takes with profound seriousness the vocation of this world's powers to serve the economy of God, in the context of the reign and promise of One who was crucified by these powers and now is their saving Lord as well as ours. To say no to those forms of power which we can develop but shouldn't, to say yes to those which serve a human purpose, and to distinguish them in the light of the humanity of Christ is the special mission of a church that bears witness to the quality of human relations in the context of a redeemed creation, which God has promised to all humanity.

# Conclusion:
# The Substance of Hope

Faith, says the letter to the Hebrews, "is the substance of things hoped for, the evidence of things not seen." (Hebrews 11:1, KJV) In all these pages we have been talking about the perspective of faith. The truth of history is God's covenant faithfulness and promise in the form of the servant, crucified and risen Christ. It is God in Christ who reconciles the world and creates human community among all our pluralities, who turns the powers of the world despite themselves into the service of justice and humanity. In Christ the powers of sin and death are already overcome. We look forward to Christ's coming again in judgment and in grace when this reality and this promise will be fulfilled. What, then, is "the substance of things hoped for" in the century and the millenium to come? How is the hope we have in the risen and coming Christ related to the secular hopes that give provisional meaning to human lives in our society?

The world has lost its great ideologies, and with them, its great hopes. They were hopes based on "science," on the "laws of history," and therefore on

human planning and control. This planning and control persists in science, technology and in global eco-
nomic-political systems. It produces results, but it
generates as much suspicion and doubt as faith and
hope; Whose interests are served by these systems?
Are they really under control or do they control their
managers? Is any goal of human welfare being pursued? Are the resources of God's creation being
responsibly used? It often appears that the whole of
this economy is the result of private decisions by many
people pursuing many goals, weighted by the wealth
and power they bring to the process. Meanwhile other
goals and other hopes—of individuals, communities,
and even nations—try to find whatever form of self-
assertion they can. Hopes, like meanings, are fragile
and fragmented in a postmodern world.

Christians in such a world have a new work to do:
to inspire the world not with ideology, but with hope.
What it means for our cultures that hope is in Christ
always at work in history, but that its reach and the
source of its truth lie beyond any historical fulfillment,
we are called to think through and spell out. We know
that God will not fulfill our economic or technological
dreams for an ever greater expansion of human prosperity and power. The end will be a time of judgment
on self-generated human ambitions and hopes. But it
will also be a time when the deepest human longings,
for forgiveness and community in love, will be realized.
Human destiny has the form of Christ the servant, the
crucified and the risen Lord. The world can depend on
that truth. God's reconciliation of the world is working
to weave society together despite the self-centered
conflicting structures of human life. The communities

of the world can find their fulfillment there. It is the vocation of the world powers to serve the economy of God, in the context of One who was crucified by these powers and now is their saving Lord. The people of the world can face the future in this confidence. Of this truth, of this community, and of this power we are witnesses, "God making his appeal through us."

# References Cited

Adams, Daniel J. 1997. Toward a Theological Understanding of Postmodernity. *Metanoia* 7, no. 1.

Arendt, Hannah. 1963. *On Revolution*. New York: Viking Press.

Barth, Karl. 1956. *Church Dogmatics*. Vol. I, Part 2. Edinburgh: T. & T. Clark.

———. 1957. *The Word of God and the Word of Man*. New York: Harper.

———. 1960. *The Humanity of God*. Richmond: John Knox Press.

———. 1973. *Protestant Theology in the Nineteenth Century*. Valley Forge, Pa.: Judson Press.

Bauman, Zygmunt. 1992. *Intimations of Postmodernity*. London: Routledge & Kegan Paul.

Berdyaev, Nicholas. 1936. *The Meaning of History*. London: G. Bles.

Bloch, Ernst. 1964. *The Principle of Hope*. Cambridge: MIT Press.

Bohr, Niels. 1958. *Atomic Physics and Human Knowledge*. New York: John Wiley & Sons.

Bonhoeffer, Dietrich. 1972. *Letters and Papers from Prison*. New York: Macmillan.

——. 1978. *Christ the Center*. New York: Harper & Row.

——. 1989. *Schöpfung und Fall*. Gütersloh: Chr. Kaiser Verlag.

——. 1992. *Ethik*. Gütersloh: Chr. Kaiser Verlag.

——. 1997. *Creation and Fall*. Minneapolis: Fortress Press.

Bosch, David. 1986. *Transforming Mission*. Maryknoll, N.Y.: Orbis Books.

——. 1995. *Believing in the Future*. Valley Forge, Pa.: Trinity Press International.

Calvin, John. 1961. *The Institutes of the Christian Religion*. Philadelphia: Westminster Press.

Descartes, René. 1958. Discourse on Method. In *Philosophical Writings*. New York: Random House.

Foster, Michael. 1934. The Christian Doctrine of Creation and the Rise of Modern Science. *Mind* 34:446–58.

Gutierrez, Gustavo. 1973. *A Theology of Liberation*. Maryknoll, N.Y.: Orbis Books.

Hauerwas, Stanley, and William H. Willimon. 1989. *Resident Aliens*. Nashville: Abingdon Press.

Hobbes, Thomas. 1914. *Leviathan*. London: J. M. Dent.

Hodge, Charles. 1981. *Systematic Theology*. Vol. I. Grand Rapids: Eerdmans.

Hromadka, Josef L. 1950. The Church of the Reformation Faces Today's Challenges. *Theology Today* 6.

Hume, David. 1967. *Treatise on Human Nature*. Oxford: Clarendon Press.

Hunsberger, George R. and Craig van Gelder. 1996. *Church Between Gospel and Culture*. Grand Rapids: Eerdmans.

Kant, Immanuel. 1938. *Critique of Pure Reason*. London: Macmillan.

——. 1964. Beantwortung der Frage: was ist Aufklärung? In *German Essays I: Was ist Aufklärung?*, edited by V.C. Hubbs. New York: Macmillan.

Kittel, Gerhard, ed. 1932: *Theologisches Wörterbuch des neuen Testaments*. Vol. I. Stuttgart: Kohlhammer.

Marx, Karl. 1964. *On Religion*. New York: Schocken Books.

——. 1978. *The Marx-Engels Reader*. Edited by R.C. Tucker. New York.: W. W. Norton.

Mott, John R. 1911. *The Evangelization of the World in This Generation*. New York: YMCA.

Newbigin, J. Lesslie. 1986. *Foolishness to the Greeks*. Grand Rapids: Eerdmans.

——. 1989. *Gospel in a Pluralist Society*. Grand Rapids: Eerdmans.

Niebuhr, H. Richard. 1956. *The Kingdom of God in America*. Hamden, Conn.: Shoe String.

Niebuhr, Reinhold. 1947. *Moral Man and Immoral Society*. New York: Scribners.

——. 1979. *An Interpretation of Christian Ethics*. New York: Seabury Press.

O'Donovan, Oliver. 1996. *The Desire of Nations*. New York: Oxford University Press.

Paton, David M. and Charles C. West, eds. 1969. *The Missionary Church in East and West*. London: SCM Press.

Paul VI. 1976. On the Development of Peoples. In *The Gospel of Peace and Justice: Catholic Social Teachings Since Pope John*. Maryknoll, N.Y.: Orbis Books.

Polanyi, Michael. 1964. *Personal Knowledge*. Chicago: University of Chicago Press.

Popper, Karl. 1952. *The Open Society and Its Enemies.* London: Routledge & Kegan Paul.

Presbyterian Church (USA). 1991. *The Book of Confessions.* Louisville: Westminster/John Knox Press.

Preston, Ronald H., ed. 1971. *Technology and Social Justice.* Valley Forge, Pa.: Judson Press.

Sanneh, Lamin. 1990. *Translating the Message.* Maryknoll, N.Y.: Orbis Books.

——. 1993. *Encountering the West.* Maryknoll, N.Y.: Orbis Books.

Scherer, James A., and Stephen B. Behrens, eds. 1994. *New Directions in Mission and Evangelization.* Vol. I. Maryknoll, N.Y.: Orbis Books.

Schleiermacher, Friedrich. 1988. *On Religion.* Cambridge: Cambridge University Press.

Smith, Adam. 1976. *The Theory of Moral Sentiments.* Oxford: Clarendon Press.

——. 1978. *The Wealth of Nations.* Oxford: Clarendon Press.

Stewart, John W. 1998. *Mediating the Center.* Princeton: Theological Seminary Press.

Van Leeuwen, Arend. 1964. *Christianity in World History.* London: Edinburgh House.

Von Rad, Gerhard. 1956. *Genesis: A Commentary.* Philadelphia: Westminster Press.

Von Weizsäcker, Carl Friedrich. 1952. *The World View of Physics.* London: Routledge and Kegan Paul.

West, Charles C., ed. 1959. *The Meaning of the Secular: Report of a Conference at the Ecumenical Institute, Bossey.* Céligny, Switzerland: Ecumenical Institute.

World Council of Churches. 1948. *The Church and the Disorder of Society: Amsterdam Assembly Series.* Vol. III. New York: Harper.

——. 1956. *Statements of the World Council of Churches on Social Questions: 1948–1955.* Geneva: World Council of Churches.

——. 1966. *World Conference on Church and Society: Official Report.* Geneva: World Council of Churches.

——. 1968. *The Uppsala Report.* Geneva: World Council of Churches.

——. 1979. *Faith and Science in an Unjust World.* 2 vols. *Report of the World Conference on Faith, Science and the Future, Cambridge, Mass., U.S.A.* Geneva: World Council of Churches.

Yoder, John Howard. 1984. *The Priestly Kingdom.* Grand Rapids: Eerdmans.

——. 1994. *The Royal Priesthood.* Grand Rapids: Eerdmans.